D0457285

# THE LAST THING

# THE LAST
# THING
NEW & SELECTED POEMS

# PATRICK
# ROSAL

A Karen & Michael Braziller Book
PERSEA BOOKS / NEW YORK

Persea Books, Inc.
90 Broad Street
New York, New York 10004

Library of Congress Cataloging-in-Publication Data
Names: Rosal, Patrick, 1969– author.
Title: The last thing : new & selected poems / Patrick Rosal.
Description: New York : Persea Books, [2021] | "A Karen & Michael Braziller Book." | Summary:
    "New poems by Patrick Rosal, along with generous selections from his first four collections"
    Provided by publisher.
Identifiers: LCCN 2021018227 | ISBN 9780892555321 (hardcover)
Subjects: LCGFT: Poetry.
Classification: LCC PS3618.O774 .L37 2021 | DDC 811/.6—dc23
LC record available at https://lccn.loc.gov/2021018227

Book design and composition by Rita Lascaro
Typeset in Cheltenham

Manufactured in the United States of America. Printed on acid-free paper.

*This book is dedicated*
*to the memory of my mother, Simeona Gelacio Rosal*

*who, with curiosity and acceptance and love,*
*watched how hard it was for the world to change,*

*and who, with and without discretion, taught me*
*how not to be full of shit,*

*and to my father, Nicholas Llanes Rosal*
*who has dared to learn*

*the incomplete and imperfect*
*language of forgiveness*

# CONTENTS

*A Preface*                                                                    xi

## NEW POEMS / \POEMAS NUEVOS / \BARO A DANDANIW / \BAGONG TULA

Boys' Bodies in Flight (are also a kind of text)                                5
A Town Called Sadness                                                          14
The Changing Hymn (Allegory of the Singing Lover)                             17
Making Out on a Hill Overlooking the Hudson                                    23
The Hanged Ghost                                                               26
A Memory on the Eve of the Return of the U.S. Military to
    Subic Bay                                                                   28
Learning to Slaughter                                                          30
If All My Relationships Fail and I Have No Children Do I Even
    Know What Love Is                                                           32
When Prince Was Filipino                                                       34
On the Elevation of Earthlings—a Hymn                                          36
Atang: Building My First Altar                                                 38
Check, Incantation Composed on the Occasion of Being
    Classified As Inadmissible                                                  41
Gift                                                                           49
Where the Ocean Ends                                                          52
La Época en que Hay Olvido                                                     54
Sleeping Animal                                                               56
The Last Thing or Song for When They Take It All Away                          58

## SELECTED POEMS

### from *UPROCK HEADSPIN SCRAMBLE AND DIVE* (2003)

B-Boy Infinitives                                                             71
Freddie                                                                       73
Nine Thousand Outlines                                                        74

You Clubhouse Boys · 76
The Next Hundred-Odd Half-Dreamed Miles · 78
Citrus City · 80
Who Says the Eye Loves Symmetry · 82
*"My Mother Is in Los Angeles"* · 83
Uncommon Denominators · 85
Poem · 87
Pick-up Line Ending with a Prayer · 88

## from *MY AMERICAN KUNDIMAN* (2006)

Meditations on the Eve of My Niece's Birth · 93
On Our Long Road Trip Home I Don't Ask My Friend if He Thinks
   His Youngest Daughter Might Be Someone Else's Kid · 94
Beast · 96
Lapu Lapu's Envoy Conveys His Response to Magellan · 98
When You Haven't Made Love in a Long Time · 99
The Woman You Love Cuts Apples For You · 100
Kundiman In Medias Res · 102
Kundiman on a Dance Floor Called Guernica · 103
Kundiman Ending on a Theme from T La Rock · 105
Kundiman for My Lover Beside Me on the Floor
   (Her Daughter Asleep on My Bed) · 107
Poem for My Extra Nipple · 108
About the White Boys Who Drove By a Second Time to
   Throw a Bucket of Water on Me · 109
As Glass · 111
St. Patrick · 114
Two Black People and a Filipino Near the Concessions
   Geraldine R. Dodge Poetry Festival · 116
Photo of My Grandmother Running Toward Us on a
   Beach in Ilokos · 117

## from *BONESHEPHERDS* (2011)

Boneshepherds' Lament · 121
Delenda Undone · 124
Little Men with Fast Hands · 126

Bienvenida: Santo Tomás 127

Tamarind 130

Crew Love Elegy 132

Sundiata Elegy 134

Ars Poetica: After a Dog 137

Naima 141

Aubade: The Monday Bargain 145

Making Love to You the Night They Take Your Father to Prison 147

Guitar 151

Despedida Ardiente 153

The Tradition of Pianos 155

## from *BROOKLYN ANTEDILUVIAN* (2016)

Despedida: Brooklyn to Philly 161

Typhoon Poem 163

At the Tribunals 165

A Scavenger's Ode to the Turntable (aka a Note to
   Thomas Alva Edison) 167

Brokeheart: Just Like That 169

Ode to the Cee-Lo Players 171

The Halo-Halo Men: An Anthem 173

Violets 175

Wish 177

Kundiman: Hung Justice 179

Instance of an Island 181

Ten Years After My Mom Dies I Dance 184

Children Walk on Chairs to Cross a Flooded Schoolyard 186

Ode to Eating a Pomegranate in Brooklyn 188

You Cannot Go to the God You Love with Your Two Legs 189

Brooklyn Antediluvian 190

*Acknowledgments* 205

# A PREFACE

*It is a human love, I live inside.*
　　　　—Amiri Baraka, "An Agony. As Now."

There's a video of the late, great Cuban percussionist, Tata Güines, giving a demonstration of Afro-Cuban music—and the role of the drums popularly called congas—to students in Bordeaux, France, 1991. The drums have many names, depending on their size and function in an ensemble. In Cuba, they are often generally referred to as *tumbadoras*.

On stage with Tata Güines is a Spanish-speaking companion (and another man off screen translating the two men's presentation into French). Tata Güines's compañero urgently but respectfully interrupts the percussion maestro to clarify for their audience the terminology and naming of the drums. The man speaks deliberately and emphatically:

> [La palabra *tumbadora*] tiene su antecedente fonético en el grupo lingüístico Bantú en África. Viene un término: *mmm-bah*. De mmm-bah viene tummm-bah [tumba]. Y de tum-mm-bah viene tummm–mmm-bah–doh–rah y es así que queda el orígen fonético africano *en el medio* de la palabra castellana—casi imperceptible.[1]

✳

My grandfather was a laborer in the sugar cane fields on the windward side of the Big Island, Hawai'i, during the late 1920s and early 30s. Apolonio Gelacio was a sakada, a manong. He cut sugar cane for a pittance. He was referred to by a number—a bango, as it was known, #936—a referent for the Hawaiian Sugar Planters Association to keep very specific track of his production, his wages, and his expenses and arrears.

In America, those sugar fields are often called canebrake, which ostensibly refers to the breaking and processing of cane so it's suitable for

---

1 "[The word *tumbadora*] has its phonetic antecedent in the Bantu language group in Africa. We get the expression *mmm-bah*; out of *mmm-bah* we get *tummm-bah* [tumba in Spanish, tomb or grave in English]; and from tummm-bah we get tumm–mmm-bah–doh–rah. And that's how an African phonetic origin in the middle of a Castilian word remains—almost imperceptible."

consumption, but I imagine it was also a place to break the wills of laborers.

My grandfather, like other sakadas, would buy many of his supplies, medicine, and whatever else he needed at the end of the week from the plantation store. And these Filipino workers were often charged the balance of their weekly wages, on top of which a poll tax was exacted, which left them with very little in terms of actual earnings; often, it left them in debt. My uncle tells me that the sakadas spent grueling hours planting and harvesting, swinging a machete at the stalk's root—hundreds and hundreds over the course of a day—and bearing the heavy bundles back and forth for transport. The crops were a visible measure of their productivity for which they were pitifully remunerated and treated like shit.

So, what my grandfather and the other manongs did was plant their own micro crops in between the rows of cane. I can imagine long beans doing well in those fields, maybe even okra or squash, maybe sweet potato too—not just for the tubers, but for the leaves and hearty stems. And maybe the men fed each other from those illicit gardens, then gathered in a bunkhouse in Pahoa to barter their greens for rum or cigarettes or a good knife. And I'm sure, there, in between the rows, beyond the direct gaze of the bosses, they didn't just plant seeds and reap their fruit, they also gossiped and cursed. They dreamt. They danced. I'm sure they sang. My uncle told me that my grandfather became a great practitioner of the Philippine stick fighting art, arnis—known as kimat in Ilokano, which means *lightning*. There, in between the thick grasses whose fibers would be processed to become the innocuous sweetness of tables across the continent of America, my grandfather and his comrades literally learned to fight for their lives—casi imperceptible.

*

Here's what I have come to learn: a system will construct a language or a field. And inside that strategically fixed construction, its subjects are expected to abide by the order of the given system.

But those very subjects will learn to do whatever they can in order to eat and fight and laugh and mourn and survive. And so, though largely illegible to those who are invested in the integrity and perpetuity of that same system—right smack in the middle of the emblems of its power—a recurring form emerges: the cultivation of the shapeshifting, elusive, lethal, polyglottal, elaborate, sometimes gorgeous improvisations of material-at-hand. And such improvisations require a plethora of qualities and skills—observation, curiosity, gathering, experimentation, collaboration, concealment, nerve, deception, discretion, wit, among others. We make a living out of the things a system prohibits, refuses, denigrates, and throws away. We study everything.

*

As a boy I felt the pressure of language, which is the pressure and illusion of containment, not just the pressure of proper pronunciation and usage, but the pressure to conform to a language's portrayals of my world, of me. Over time, I believed that one of two things would happen: the pressure (of a name, a word, a category) would either break me or I would have to find the fracture in the container and bust the fuck out. I chose—naively, romantically—the latter. Little did I know, the box remakes itself. The box is regenerative . . . But so, too, are its fissures. And one way to begin to break any box open from the inside is to bang on the walls and listen to its faults. Even if I couldn't crack the box, the banging made a music that couldn't be contained.

And one might go as far to theorize that the sounds I have made change the space that encloses me. Some might say that space is America. That theory might or might not prove to be true. The manongs' exuberantly secret disobedience between the cane rows did not grind the sugar industry to a halt. Nor did our linguistic creolizations in the Americas and Africa and the Pacific extract or eradicate the Iberian idiom from our governance or names or song. Not in any clear or absolute way, anyway.

Sure, it could be that the history of making, its infinitely complex processes, and all its imperfect objects have instigated some change in the world. Personally, I can't say for sure. The only change I can attest to is my own imagination. There's nothing special about this change—nothing politically radical, but actually something quite natural.

The poetic principle that says a field of industrial crops can be turned into a dance floor and that a Spanish word for drum can be turned into an invocation to ancestors is also a principle that suggests, that a sinner is not simply a sinner because a society and its systems need a sinner, nor is a king simply a king, nor is a thief just a thief. And none remains any one thing forever. For example, tomorrow they could all be a river.

*

Ritual, the encoding of memory into the body by sound and movement, communication with the dead and the yet-to-be-born, "performances" in which everyone present is invited to participate, call and response, the appropriation and reinvention/recontextualization of a widely disseminated or familiar artifact, the fragment as compositional element, the fundamental practice of observing and getting to know the land and material that are right in front of you, keening, feeling as a route to and from the imagination, feeling in collaboration with reason, the juxtaposition of unlikely elements or objects, a spirit of play, the revelation of the expressive potential of something commonplace, the fluid boundary between storytelling and song—these are not innovative artistic practices, let alone entrepreneurial opportunities; these modes are so old. These modes of study were preserved and reinvented by many who came before me. And my job as an artist—as I see it—is to preserve and reinvent the soul of those modes and practices to the best of my attention and skill and love.

I like to believe if I listen close enough, I might hear what we all used to be; I like to believe we might briefly grasp what we might become. A practice of justice must contain within it a sense of the certainty that things and people can and will change, and a sense of justice must also contain the uncertainty of who, what, where, how, and why...

I suppose I keep writing and making music and art because somewhere in our attention to this uncertainty we ourselves are changed. And just as important, we might catch a glimpse of a genesis, which is both heartbreaking and hilarious.

And that might be the first and last thing that ever really matters.

*Tenez je ne suis plus qu'un homme, aucune dégradation, aucun crachat
ne le conturbe, je ne suis plus qu'un homme qui accepte n'ayant plus de
colère (il n'a plus dans le cœur que de l'amour immense, et qui brûle)*

*J'accepte . . . j'accepte . . . entièrement, sans réserv . . .*
　　　　　　—AIMÉ CÉSAIRE


　　　　　　　*. . . ready*
　　*for the fire*
　　　　　　—WILLIAM CARLOS WILLIAMS

# THE LAST THING

NEW POEMS / \ POEMAS NUEVOS / \ BARO A DANDANIW / \ BAGONG TULA

# Boys' Bodies in Flight (are also a kind of text)

*Boys don't read.*
      —the experts

These kids run
their sloppy fly routes

right to left
in a crabgrass park

They are counting
by the thousands They read

the defense and cheat the rush
or jump the snap

One of them eats a nice
blindside hit

from a slightly older bigger kid
and buckles for half a second

then jumps to his feet
You might not notice

the big kid brush
the shorter one's shoulders

before he shoves the littler guy
good and hard and hustles

toward the huddle
                    When I was
their age there were days

no one for nine blocks
could come out to play

So I used to ride my bike
to Grace Street and sit alone

in the middle of the baseball field
standing up once in a while

to pitch dirt bombs at the church's
back wall
        its glass stained

with the lean long-robed
saints of Bonhamtown

and a few undecipherable
aphorisms of the Roman faith

        Among my first urges
toward ruin: to crack open

an enclosure holy or not
and set free

what might roost inside
I'd imagine slinging a rock

through one of the saint's heads
and a plague of grackles

streaming from the breach
the birds rushing out a lot like

gangs of brawling boys do
spilling across an Avenue

underneath a second-floor
neon Szechuan sign

How many times I was swift
to headbutt another kid in the chin

or moosh some brat in the face
who I thought was breathing

too hard and too close at the bar
and so with a quick swat

I could set a whole downtown
plaza ablaze with crews

of crackling boys pouncing
upon each other
                Under streetlamps

I bet we looked like jackdaws
stomping out flames or rooks

simply mauling smaller birds

Someone told me

                the key to peace
is learning to make my mind

still as a field—like maybe
the one from my childhood

with its crumbling backstop
across from the abandoned

cosmetics warehouse
I've often wondered

if the jagged painted glass
of Grace Street Church

is finally nailed shut
with some cheap chipboard

I keep thinking the roof
has probably collapsed by now

but I'm really remembering a shrine
near my mom's hometown

that was bombed
by Americans

who thought the enemy
was hiding inside

When the townspeople came
to see the damage

there was a real sky
in the gaping space left

in place of the original sky
frescoed on the dome
                which had fallen in

More wondrous: the attack
knocked loose a huge

statue from its perch
The ten-foot saint

cut from local stone
landed on its feet

and was poised at the center
of the altar and thus

forever blessed the site
with enough power

to invoke a pilgrimage
by the grown sons and daughters

of the nation's latest dictator
They knelt before that hard white figure

to request their several intercessions
sobbing prostrate and surrounded

by men strapped with Armalites
By then the local engineers

and artists had been called
to fix the image of Heaven

the shadows of small black birds
now fleeing paradise

along the sunray's
golden angles of descent

I was brought up
on the other side of the planet

in a Jersey neighborhood
whose one field

was quiet long enough
to bear the silence

of a seventy-five-year-old church
and a solitary nine-year-old boy

testing his scrawny arm
and the inherited pleasures

of rage I was twenty-five
when my mother died

It would be several years
before she came back

for a quick visit  We met
in that field by our old house

A bare maple lay on its side
between us She somehow figured out

I was hungry
so she turned to a line of bushes

near the crown of the fallen timber
and whistled

Three notes into my mother's call
out burst a half dozen

fluttering game quail
so quick to flight

they impaled  themselves
on the bare branches

of the fallen tree
My mom held out her arms

as if to call my attention
to the flapping bloody fruit

There are no photos of my mother
before 1958

the year she arrived in America
I think as a child she must have been

very much like the children
in our ancestral village

who once accompanied me
to the family cemetery Even there

these children dart from grave to grave
reciting their own names

and the distant years carved
by hand They leap

from one hard marker to another
laughing in brigades

               They laugh
like hundreds of flocks

once locked up in some musty space
made sacred

by so many small bodies
crashing into glass
               Doesn't everyone

know of boys who dream
repeatedly of wings
                    And yet

so few of us know what to tell them
the morning they wake up

and feel what it's like
to be changed by pain

Every generation there's another kid
on the wrong side of the world

who stops praying in a dusty field
to lift a stone so he can begin

to understand what it's like
to wish for the same thing

for the rest of his life
promising

to spring every body
of every ghost

from every shackle
and every old wood hold

It took me decades
to salvage my sadness

from books Tell me again
that boys don't read

It is their hothead fathers
and stubborn uncles

who are too terrified to listen
let alone inscribe the fleeting

stories that would name the first
secret agony of those little bones

poking through their backs

# A Town Called Sadness

On the fifth day of heartbreak
driving 800 miles to the desert
I pulled into Sadness
I parked slantways across two stalls
lost as ever and checked the map
for something familiar
I'd rolled into the lot
of what looked like a hotel
this big blonde brick building
maybe five stories tall
every window the same except for one
flung wide open with a man
shoved half way through
wearing a tank top stretched
just past his bellybutton
and a good six-day scruff on his chin
*Get in here Diane!* he barked
*Bring your ass inside!* And Diane
—she must have been 11 or so—
stood in sagging socks
just two parking spots down
staring into the blacktop
I think she knew what I knew too:
The day sucked  Even the sky
looked like secondhand cotton
smeared with cheap mascara
but here's the kicker—Diane's right
fist was shoved inside the bold bright bell
of a big shiny French horn
Its tubes and curves wound
toward her mouth She'd figured out
how not to let it slip from her hip
and it was gleaming so hard
this bad overcast hanging above us all—
cantankerous windbag included—
conceded some of the day's space

to this one hunch-shouldered child
clutching a little dazzling galaxy
of voluptuous metal

Some of us are lucky enough to arrive
at Sadness with our eyes open
Some of us are born there
with lungs enough to blow
It's as good as any place
to put silver to your lips
and kiss the world with a blare
even when the world's got it out for you
even if you're wearing knee socks
tore up kicks and an ill-fitting skirt
that isn't designed after the sky
In Sadness the sky's the design
You don't even have to pull it over your head
I wasn't supposed to get my heart broke
I wasn't supposed to fuck it up
I wasn't supposed to say good night

I don't know why I didn't stay
long enough to see if Diane
got her ass inside
or if she walked away
I like to think she went on
blasting the most curvaceous
brass passage she wanted to practice
all afternoon daring someone anyone
to come and drag her back
I dropped my car into gear
and sped out onto the highway
I made it to the city limits
I passed the exit for Hope
I made my way to the desert
It was just one day of course

but it was the day I counted myself
smart enough to stop in a town
I couldn't find on any map
It was the day I got moving soon enough
that there was no end to joy

# The Changing Hymn (Allegory of the Singing Lover)

*For Mary Rose*

During the Trouble Years
my love sang the same song
every day but every day
she'd change—slightly—the words
One day she sang a song for sweepers
and the next day the sweepers became
hangmen On Friday the hangmen turned
into willows In September
the willows turned back to broomsticks
broken in the hands of janitors
She and I used to play a game
waiting for the ferry or on long walks
to my auntie's house One of us
would begin a song
and the other would repeat the line
changing just one word—
back and forth like that—
drawing and redrawing the images
in the lyrics each time growing
an extra eye or tongue or
losing a foot one word at a time
The game gave us nuns (whom we loved)
on skateboards and who ate steamed buns
in Muncie where they confessed
to the Best Western desk
they were once boys who were once
orchids who were snakes first
slithering through midtown palaces
blazing on trains turned
rocketships in Oxnard and tractors in Parlin
before straddling massive salamanders
in Paris where the sisters farted
on the heads of billionaires
and shook tambourines
in their yellow teeth before

they got down on their knees and prayed
And the cold mist of the ferry was
always good And the cold air between
our house and my auntie's just as good

My darling loved most to sing
in dark places especially dank bars
packed with locals who were swift
to rise from their crummy chairs
and stagger to their feet setting their drinks
on the closest table or they'd simply
fling their glasses to the floor
to finally hold one another so close
they could sniff each other's cheeks
though hardly anyone knew another's name
My love put their tables in her song
and the backroom's musty wood
and the dusty lavender smell of factories
beside the perfume of goat breath
like a gift inside the song
and sometimes the crowd
would swell into laughter all together
to see if such a singer and such a song
could hold the joyful sound
of a hundred strangers and
they would stomp and twirl
to see if their dance
could keep up with my love's song
and with all their singing and swinging
stepping and sliding they forgot
their walking legs and their meat hooks
and the thick pine smell
that haunted their saws
my lover's song so fearless
sometimes the dead got up too
for even the most crotchety of our elders knew

if we opened ourselves up
wide enough to the song
the song would not leave us
even lying down
                        and this is how
her singing became a country
that could go everywhere
a vagabond that moved through
whoever welcomed it This is how
a song became a little nation
inside a hundred people
grooving so hard no one could say
exactly what a nation was—the land
the people upon it or the ones
buried in its fields and hills
for the dancers were pure tremor
cycle and vibration Migrants
they were pure wave

Sometimes short on rent my love
would sing for quick money
in big beautiful halls    crystalline and sad
where the people were also sad
for their ties were always straight
and their clothes were well pressed
and they dared not scuff the good gleam
of their belt buckles—that kind of sad—
they were so rich with the wealth of silks
and platinum garland and fast boats
The marble floors of their salons
so clean you couldn't tell a single
blade was put to wood
or that a drop of blood had fallen
on their shiny tiles
                        No evidence
of the making

                but by god
when my love sang every one of these
bright-buttoned folks would sway
barely budging at first
so you couldn't notice the ghosts
stirring inside them
like a sugar starting to cook
into its first kick of liquor     swirling now
nudging them like a sweet inner fog
They tried (Oh did they try) not
to let the rhythm in     They gripped
the tables' silver in their fingers
and curled their toes inside their shoes
And just as the music got into their stiff hips
their bodies relented     It was then
my love would begin to fit new words
to this familiar tune     And clever
she would hide me inside the song(!)
maybe just the crook of my neck
or the pink scar across my forehead
(which she'd touch to calm me
when I was sick) Sometimes
she'd smuggle into the song
my busted up pinky     my bruised feet
or my father's piano     And I would laugh
even louder when the coiffed ones laughed
so hard and loose they seemed
to be breaking all their great grandfathers' rules
for even the powerful understand
the power of what's hidden
how a woman's voice of wild harps
and charging horses was guiding
this monster of a song inside them
while all us  savages and outcasts
rode stowaway tucked into the tune
with all our fists and all our feet

and all our sweat and grime
soiling their powdered armpits
and fancy panties in public

And when my love finished
they would suddenly close up like
a patient quickly suturing himself shut
At the end of the night
their long candles burned to their bit wicks
a few of them would approach my love
and shake her hand as if
she had only one arm They'd thank her
as if she had no eyes to kiss
and she would tell me going home
she knew the song would not
stay inside them the way it seemed to abide
in us that spirit which makes
the hammer and hoe blade ring
and the hospital's faucet water
so cool to the lips you might lick the spigot
and the engine of the trolley rattle hot
this very old spark of the body working
and working and working
              it all on out

And there were mornings—though awake—
my love would lie in bed like empty luggage
For many nights she moaned in her sleep
as if the song were leaving her for good too
But then in a week or month      often
after the winter cold lost its sting
to the first gingko buds
we'd lift our heads at the same time
and hear a small breaking
                          the cracking
of a crate smashed glass and crystal

which gave way to flutes and cuckoos
the heavy steps of old ghosts
to keep the new ghosts company
This widening country of wandering bodies
all the sound  through which she roamed
and every sound which roamed within us
she made and unmade and remade again
in the Trouble Time      everything
she sang and unsang out of fevers and blood
where no one was ever lonely
          She never wanted others to be lonely
She sang so no one would ever
be lonely
            I'm speaking in the past
as if we will never exist again
                  and yet
                              every song changes
as it goes        We've already begun
to turn into tomorrow
            We are the soonest sounds to come

# Making Out on a Hill Overlooking the Hudson

Above the boulevards of sweat
where the kids    are gathering again

at the back    of a public bus
to plan    the resurrection    of laughter

an old woman    on a bench    slides
both pink shoes    off her feet
at the beginning of spring

so she can sit    a while longer
and look    at the same river    as us

As if she needs a little extra heat
she rubs    her hands together    so vigorously
the jays all leap    at once

I could stop the sun right now
I could be wicked    as a fruit thief

I could touch your middle knuckle    with my thumb
and pretend    I don't know    all your names

but    the cherry blossoms are just coming    into view

From the heights    old men    secretly wish
to leap    into their creamy    bloom

Logic tells them    *Patience Friend    Wait
another year*    It took a long time

for you and I    to follow the river
back    to where it kills

and Nature    isn't the only    murderer
to go free    but at least    it's got a million
tasks for the tongue

so when    two mouths    come together
they only mean    to stand    for emptiness

They redraw    borders    in the smallest districts
of the body    like the passing    of an electron

from hydrogen    to hydrogen    to form
another    variation    of water These days

                    everywhere    I go
a word    I can't pronounce    begins

to sing    deep inside me    It signifies
half an absence    Your mouth signifies    another

Between the two of us    we are bearing
six languages    into the future

We share the seventh    which is silence

The century ahead of us    will want to know
how the landscapes    changed
in our brief lifetimes    I want to be clear

                    We stripped
to our ankles    once    and danced

We catalogued    each vibrant thing
beside a dying river    at dusk

We became     whatever we named
We were     so sick     from suffering
we pressed our lips
                              to everything
        we could not bless

# The Hanged Ghost

*for my great uncles*
*Mamerto, Nicasio, Prudencio Llanes*
*who were hanged by the U.S. military*
*for their armed resistance against*
*the American occupation of the Philippines*


Who am I?          I

slide my body        into
your body                    all my weight
yours        I place the gnawed
          peach pits of my ankles
into your ankles


                    I'm the rain
gathering in your right        ear
I'm the cold roar        of the storm


in the black burning        trees
          in the hills' cedars        It's a new
season for them        to hang
heads        from gibbets and magnolias
          and not once examine
the blue light's angle        off these
          dark eyes        off every inch
of the hand                dragged        they say
by the hooves        out of the shadows
to the edge        of a road        Afraid Yes
I'm        so afraid        On the Day of All Souls


I breeze back
                    to the churches of the living
I follow                    the hymns
to the deep caves
and feel with my fingers        for the secrets
scrawled        with great care        on their walls

Grief      Haunting      Don't the dead
also long      to be touched      in the dark

          When boys come      to shove
the small of my back      and make me swing
      so slightly
as if they could scare off      the other ghosts
to their astonishment
      touch is a kindness
      and a failure

But who will say?      Even if someone cuts me down
there will always be another      with arms wide open
to say: *here it is*      Our communion
of silence and lies Left here long enough

even the mushrooms      in time
will take me      in their double thousand
microscopic mouths

# A Memory on the Eve of the Return of the U.S. Military to Subic Bay

Every day      in America
    I am trying              to be taken
seriously
        When
    the United States          last
owned              the naval base      at Subic Bay
my uncle      (my father's      distant
    cousin)    was a colonel    in charge
      of Philippine forces      under
    Marcos      On our first      and only
visit          to  the Philippines
  my brother      (maybe      eight)
and I      (thirteen?)      were left
alone      in my uncle's      house
    with one      of my uncle's
guards      and my uncle's      grandson—
a boy          maybe five And
when the guard      dashed out
to eat lunch      he left      the front door
    open
and the five-year-old      with us
    The sentry
had slid      his gun      under a small table
beside the door              And the boy
    who spoke      no English
picked up      the automatic          and
    pointed the rifle      at my chest
then
    my brother's
        head
    The boy
      was smiling
It must have been              funny
    on the other      side
of the gun              I couldn't      simply stroll
    my little brother      past the barrel

to the door     where it was     a bright
        blue day          I couldn't see
the safety     from where     I was standing
              So I said
*Put that     down     I'm serious*
        and the boy     laughed
I said *Put it     down It's not     a joke*
        and the boy     laughed
        some more     He laughed
in the colonel's     language     and
he laughed     in mine     as if we all
understood     the laughter
              Sometimes
I think there
              are two countries
                        one
on either side              of a gun There
are guns     at the borders     but
that's how     borders     are made
They     are made     of guns
        I'm
              serious

# Learning to Slaughter

After a while I let the flies bite my legs

I never got sick of the children
singing karaoke      I wasn't amazed

when the young ones kept on cutting the air
with all the tin in their bodies
                all the rust in their bodies

The pig squealed so wide I could see
the pink ridges of the roof of its mouth

The pig kicked so hard
the four men had to let go

It kicked and kicked until
it flipped off the block into the dirt

My cousin touched the spot
along the neck with his fingertips

as if there were no knife
to push hard through the hide

A girl waited on her haunches
holding a bowl to catch the blood

I stopped speaking to anybody
and that was the closest I got to prayer

I put down the knife
It was just a matter of time

before the music started again
though the children were well into the second chorus

I let myself weep openly in the unpaved street
The amateur muggers and sommeliers

of cheap rum didn't even sneer
as they skipped over my ankles

I knew forgiveness: The children stopped
      for nothing
not even the strange sobbing of an uncle

My aunt said *Enough*
and it was enough

The men brought buckets to wash away the blood

When they were done
            the water was so clear

you could sip it from someone else's hands

## If All My Relationships Fail and I Have No Children Do I Even Know What Love Is

This fireman comes every afternoon
to the café on the corner
dressed for his shift in clean dark blues
This time      it's the second Wednesday of January
and he's meeting his daughter again
who must be five or six
and who is always waiting for her father like this
in her charcoal gray plaid skirt
with green and red stripes
She probably comes here straight from school
her glasses a couple nickels thick

By now I know      that she can sit      (except
for her one leg swinging from the chair)
absolutely still      while her father pulls
fighters' wraps from his work bag
and begins half way down the girl's forearm
winding the fabric in overlapping spirals
slowly toward her fist      then      he props
her wrist      like a pro      on his own hand
unraveling the black cloth      weaving it
between her thumb and forefinger
around the palm      taut but
not so much that it cuts off the blood      then
up the hand and between the other fingers
to protect the knuckles      the tough
humpback guppies just under the skin

He does this once with her left      then again
to her right      To be sure her pops knows he has done
a good job      she nods      *Good job      Good*
Maybe you're right      I don't know what love is
A father kisses the top of his daughter's head
and knocks her glasses cockeyed
He sits back and downs the last of the backwash
in his coffee cup      They got 10 minutes to kill

before they walk across the street       down the block
and out of sight       She wants to test
her dad's handiwork       by throwing
a couple jab-cross combos from her seat
There is nothing in the daughter's face
that says       she is afraid
There is nothing in the father's face
to say he is not                He checks his watch
then holds up his palms       as if to show his daughter
that nothing is burning              In Philadelphia
there are fires       I've seen those  in my lifetime too

# When Prince Was Filipino

It was 1983    I was 14 years old    the night
Charmaine Makaiyak led me    in secret
to the basement kitchen    of St. Matt's cafeteria
She put her lips    on my left earlobe
and soft-sang two choruses    of Prince's "Do Me"
so I might finally learn    how to slow dance right
Was it winter?—because    the prettiest sophomore
at the Annual    Filipino Family Gala
took my hand    and an icy wave
climbed up my banks    a blizzard wind
shook both my alleys    and all my leaves
fell off my trees

What's a bony    floppy-haired boy to do
but keep his eyes    wide open    acknowledge
the tabernacles of silence    built above him
and then open his arms
to enter the thick    religious mist
of grape hair spray    that surrounds the girl
who is    about to kiss him?

Every once in a while    it is good
for us to remember    there was one February
of the last millennium    when Prince was
Filipino    just like me    five-foot-two
in big-heel shoes    He sang so good
and played    every instrument    All the rumors
we wanted to believe    He was our Ecclesiastes
of Nasty    our Funky Future    our unrepentant
sweet    and sinful serenade

While all the grown-ups    spazzed out    to Laura Branigan
Charmaine and I convened    in the dark
tearing    at the seams    of rayon
to study the country    that history hid inside us
Every time we shifted our hips    we killed

another century        By August
they'd pop Ninoy in the skull      and drop him
bloody      on the tarmac      of Manila International
so we slow jammed      and sucked each other's lips
under the at dazzle      of a disco ball      Dawn
and dusk      I watched both Jersey skies turn
purple      OK Prince      was never Filipino      And I
was never very American      even
when I was one of two      horny kids
trying to get back      to where our parents' tropics
first burned      and so what a lucky bum I was
when Charmaine snuck me
into the room where custodians      kept all the fire
I held her until the sun      bumped through
and the heavens swelled
the color      of a busted left eye socket

Before you could type your name in light
to find where in the world      your body was hype
before fiber optic      before
we got terachomped      before we hired a machine
to court the hits

a girl let me hook      one finger
into the loop of her tight      stonewash
Jordache knockoffs
and I brushed my thumb      back and forth
over the little mile      of sweat-cooled skin
hiding under the cropped      neon tanktop
riding up her side      She taught me to move
I never went to sleep
It was 1983
America didn't know what time it was—
and neither      did we

# On the Elevation of Earthlings—a Hymn

*—To Kobe Bryant*

Kobe      a man can't make a planet
or craft a galaxy with his bare hands
but he can jab step on the wing
to juke a dude so hard out of his crouch
he bolts into a second orbit      I'm saying
a man can make whole worlds
out of a crowd's stillness      if the stillness
is the preface to awe      if the man hangs
in the air not by gallows or noose
but by his own muscle
and wish
             I once floated thirty-six-
thousand feet into the Brooklyn sky
and looked down on every cloud
above Lefferts Gardens      the Heights
Bed Stuy—Lower Merion too!
Truth is I just flew round-trip to the tropics
when I sat same row with a woman
and her six-year-old girl whose father
they lowered into the ground
not ten months earlier      The daughter clutched
one rose in each fist as if these two blooms
were the secret engines propelling
everything that leaves the earth
What a gift then      when she serenaded me
with three tunes in three languages
and both our laughter after each one

We might not know who or what
we'll meet when we get up high enough
over the ordinary rooms
into extraordinary love      but sometimes
we bear witness to a body in flight
and for a moment know what to do
with half our human sorrow

I'm only one of millions who have seen you
bang once toward the baseline then rise
before fifty thousand eyes
that stare up into the middle heavens
where your lean frame engraves a space
for a higher (though vanishing) plane
where reason and mathematics
get all the laws and formulas wrong
Just look at our faces      Kobe      We are
what singing looks like before the song

# Atang: Building My First Altar

First I set down the candle
    and place beside it a porcelain saint
of mercy    I light the wick

and twist a glass of water once
    in front of the statue
and lay down

a gift of beads Latasha gave me
    when we made music together for Sekou,
and because I'm one of the sons

who asks for forgiveness,
    I lean my mother's picture against
a tall bottle of Barbadian rum

and in front of that a glass
    with half a finger worth of its liquor
and to remember my father's Jesus

I hang a little wood cross on the wrist
    of a wood robot and for a little fortune
I place my last orange at the saint's feet.

I turn out the lights. I have no blessings.

I say thank you for the rum
    and the water and the wood of the tree
that is the body of the Robot of Waiting.

I say thank you for my mother
    and the mercy. Thank you for Latasha
and Sekou. Thank you for both the fire

and the orange who are first cousins.
  I bow my head. I don't know if there is
a direct line to God. So I make another prayer.

  And it goes like this:

*Dear Whoeveryouare,*
  *Every time I travel to an unknown place*
  *I'm sure to lose something. Today,*

  *I promise not to pray to find those things again.*
  *Instead, I pray for the dogs in my heart to sleep*

  *and for the house of my cousin built into the side of a mountain*
  *packed with rock and fire to be safe*

  *and the other cousin of the other house beside the river to be safe*
  *from poison and to be safe from flood.*

  *I pray for their presence of mind to save all their doors.*
  *I pray for my brothers and sisters, who are exiles.*

  *Everywhere I go is an unknown place,*
  *even here, where the pigeons line the wire*

  *waiting for a fat man to dump a crushed half loaf of white bread*
  *out of a clear plastic bag on the corner below my window.*

  *I pray to make my foreignness holy.*

  *Here is a bit of food I cooked myself*
  *in a tiny bamboo bowl.*

  *Dear ancestor, Dear saint,*
  *One day I will say your name.*

*Let me improvise it like a knife.*
*Let me bury it in another prayer.*

*Let me improvise it like a kite.*

*One day I'll close all my skies.*
*One day I'll be nothing but listening.*

*I'll go back to the first land I came from*
*where the whole world is unheard of,*

*where everything that is holy is strange.*

# Check, Incantation on the Occasion of Being Classified As Inadmissible

Too rowdy  for the hallowed
galleries     Too
   taciturn
for the slaughters
   Too toothsome
for daughters     Too
   couth     to dig
what's hip     Too blissful
   to moan with the crows     Nose
too wide     too flat
   too peasant Too punch-
drunk Too much muscle
   in the jaw     Too pauper Too
pansy for gangsters Not gook
   enough               Not book-
ish enough for the bland man
   standing at
the gate     Check Too     lummox
   to scuffle Too     late Too slow
for stoners     Too swift
   for varsity
track Too     slacker Too
   slant-eyed     Too brave
to bounce Too wistful
   Too bird-like
(Too many birds
   to begin with!)     Check Too
fobbish     Too fleeting
   First
I'm this     then
   suddenly     I'm that     Too
many windows
   to see into Too many skulls
to bust     Too bright
   for my own good Too fugitive

Too  gruesome Too green Not
      enough      crooning      off-
key      out of
      time Clocked      Check
the pocket Too
      solemn Too here Too
there Too queer
      In this era      every world I enter
checks a passport      And
      every room      is a world      Every crime
      a virtue            Every hunger
      sin Too corny Too      thick-lipped
and wicked-dicked
      Too horny
Too funky
      in the armpits and
ass-crack Check! Too prayerful
      Even kneeling
too potty-
      mouthed Too much
      hops for the scrubs
Not enough bunnies
      for the big-boy
courts Not lion but
      monkey Too dark
Too pissed
Too joyful Too
      prone to exuberance
and fits of mad
      dancing Too
b-boy Not Boogie-Down
      enough which is
to say too Jersey Not
      Philly enough      which is to say
too *much* New York Too
      Knickerbocker

Too giant Too thick
    in the cock Too
rooster Too rueful Too rich
    for the poor house
too poor for the White
    House Too wild
Too stylin Too
    much decibels
for the downstairs
    neighbor Too quick
with the tongue Not enough
    laughing Too fast
with the hands Not
    thief enough Not genius
enough Too dim-
    witted Too
wrathful Catholic
    Too cautious Too taut-
o-logical Not
    begotten enough Not
sorry    Not on my knees
    once more    Too doggish
Too fishy Too much
    water Not enough
meat Too tough
    Too easy to ravage
Too savage Too loose
    in the hips Too smooth
Too    mutable Too Abel
    Too Cain Too groovy
to be so goddamned
    grave Too tune-less
for conservatory Too con-
    servative Too
straight Too twisted
    Too hammered

Too screwed
    Too lifted Too bruja
    Too blessed    Too blasphemed
on the verge of a third millennium
where everyone    I profess
    to love is inclined to the same *Amen*
*Hallelujah Yes*
    I find I    have agreed    I find it all
    so    agreeable


    I begin to feel some kind of way
    I feel    a way
    This is what dissent is:    to feel
away    from myself
to travel a distance by feeling
to make some    ground by feeling    And then:
    whoso loves us    maps us out
    which is to say:    Love
is a feeling    away
    Love is a dissent
(a vexation    as in the Latin
vectus    which suggests    a carriage
    a vehicle)
    for Love is a repertoire
of migrations    And whomever you love
is an argument    an agony
a version of you
and I    a version of my Beloved
One self    multiplies and one expands
    and another    contracts into pity
into its exquisite miseries and shame
    the self    the size of a fly
    or just    one of its thousands of eyes Too
    small Not
even molecular
    and sometimes

I have migrated
far away enough from myself
    I'm alone
And even loneliness hasn't killed me
Even solitude
    has kept me Even my apartness:
a gestation for a miracle    by which
    I must simply mean    a kind of looking
        Not worship    Not muttering
in disbelief    but this week-old sheet of ice and snow
on a bright roof    beginning to melt in March
    gathering into fine streams
that split    and join again toward
    a gutter's ragged edge
where this first liquid bead    hangs
scintillating    at the brink
      dilating like one utterly gleaming    eye
through which you can see the vast
    empty destination    of a psalm
then dozens of such small glassy droplets follow
    They pause    at their limit
    then fall
one    by one    in cascading angles
    all these glistening
hesitations now that collect finally
    in a small    shallow pool
clear to last summer's muck    below my ledge    Spring
is coming    you
    idiot    You could sip
from all those eyes    Too
    many Too    thirsty
And never too    old
    for damnation    The cup
from which you drink
    is bitter (Right

I'm talking
      to myself again) Too gro-
tesque Too tramp      for sweetness      Too
      slapstick All the boats
      washed
into the streets
      by tropic floods
All the ribs of every
      hand-hewn hull      crushed Too
frail Too beggar
      for touch  Today
there are only three
of me      to go around      Too
      archipelagic      atoll
Austronesian Too
      coastal      Too
ghastly      In advance
      of dying      alert Too
dagger Too keen
      Too slick Too
trickster
      with my several
hundred ears—
      Too idle Check!
Too chill Too
      bovine      Come
kiss me      Check! Two
      good hooves one
good knee      Check
      beneath flow
Check under-
      ground      This is what
water sounds like
      at the end
of winter
      at the edge

46

of a city to which
    I've been admitted
on condition
    of my loyalty
to several
    hierarchies
of flags    Check
    Sorrow    Check yourself
for sorrow    No noose
    today    The rope's
for climbing
    Not too high
now    Too brave
    Too nimble Too
agile for perpetual
    mourning    I once
set fire
    to a whole piano
in my mother's yard
    Mother dead    Check
Too woeful Too manly
Too handsome for ransom
Too boastful    Too dark
    to spark a J or light
a candle Too devout
    Too distracted
by the little spines
    of a fish    I've done
some killing
    Someone has done
some killing
    on my behalf
I've done some
    living Too
much living
    In this country

the dream
     is the living
And for some
     the living
is too much

# Gift

When you hold
a slice

of fresh cut
red melon

to my lips
I drink

as much
as I eat

And though we give
the same name

to every incarnation
of this vine

the taste from this
one is specific

(for it must carry
the savory

hint of metal
the particular salt

of your forefinger
and thumb)

to which I say
Give me

the whole thing
the history of it

If there is a war
buried

in this gift
I'll eat that too

Like most fruit
it holds its own

water
which once was

rain or glacier
or dew extracted

and gathered
over time

after a massacre
of elk

or the slow
extinction of fish

Let me
kiss it all back

into your tongue
to say

Look
I'm real

in a world
full of figments

I didn't know grief
could cool

a fever body
but here

you and I are
taken

in each other's mouths
becoming

the temperature
of the sea

# Where the Ocean Ends

I don't know how I feel about so many masters
painting me that stupid blue and calm

as if I were not all salt     fish shit and whale scum
Doldrums Lunar collaborations Tradewinds

and crosscurrents     In your language when you say
titanic     colossal     to grasp my vastness

so do you measure my indifference
to slaughte     What

you really mean to say is deadly     Haven't you
heard me lower my voice

to lull the sentries and charm the kingmakers
and widows     Even in the Beginning

when it was just me and the bird and the sky
I didn't sing just one dumb note          Poets

love to chart those darling maps of me
with their petty thirst     gazing from the coastline

counting the seashells     each pink blip     simple
and shining in the sand like     a multitude of scars

If all my admirers could tell the difference
between righteousness and ruin

they'd do well to bear witness     to the saved
how they shut their ears and eyes

when their cousins drown     Those little gasps
and sweet orgasmic     murmurs

Oh there's evidence But who of you has the time
or courage to look    Go ahead and try

Catalog the millions of miles corroded and crystalline
I'm not a God or a mother I'm a goddamned thief

No one knows my real name        I'm so deep
you'll spend generations trying to find the bones

# La Época en que Hay Olvido

Sometimes I enter the small chambers of the God of Forgetting
and take my place at his feet
and kneel
and bow my head.

And I say into the ground that bears both of us:
*I need you—now. You*

*who have listened to the supplications*
*of tyrants, dictators*
*and kings—in my lifetime alone,*
*granted countless wishes.*

But there is already a country renamed for its suffering,
and an altar upon which
the innocent secretly
undo the knots
with their teeth.

All I have to offer are rotting carrots
and a basil plant
dying in stale water.

I used to eavesdrop on the priests who moonlight as assassins
to make sure my name
doesn't appear in their diaries.

How many people have come outside
from their desperate invocations
and self mutilation

to see the wonder for themselves? Is it true?
Are the juncos
singing
in the dogwoods?

Have the dancers removed their right shoes?
Are they hopping around
on both hands?

Yes, it *is* true. We are closing our eyes. To forecast death
we gather with strangers,
like this one woman
in the mustard coat
sitting on a park bench.

Her son has opened a small blue box stuffed with peanuts
and he pours them into her one cupped hand
so a few fall
for the sparrows
and all the while

the chainsaw is singing to each of us: STAY! STAY AS LONG AS YOU LIKE!
NO ONE CAN KEEP YOU!
and the boy—I told you—
is trying to fly.

He first lifts one wing, then lets both go. Now
watch the little one
take off

leading his enormous dragon made of water and light
by its silver leash. See

the long liquid flock of glistening muscle
ripples from the child's fist

# Sleeping Animal

From here I can see the children
running across the long field

for no other reason
than
they are fast.

*

What shall I pray for
today?

Wealth? Good looks?
Youth?

In my third life
I'm supposed to fall

into the ears
of a puma and hold

my hands up
inside the caverns

of its skull
to touch

the night songs
coming in.

Oh second life!
You were not the best,

and still how
lucky I was

to have no given map
but a language

to ask
a sleeping beast

if their teeth
still ached

after so many seasons
have passed

since
their last kill

# The Last Thing or Song for
# When They Take It All Away

—they take the books
the crates
of eighties 12-inch singles

a few dozen letters
from Manila
LA
Seville
They take

my stinky trash can
and cracked plastic chair
the rickety

plywood shelves
eleven photos of my mother

leaving me
with one
They take
the dim shots
of my brothers'
young faces beside mine
They take away

the clean sheets folded
among the soiled ones
the hand towels
stained with fevers and shit
and official
notices of all my debt
stuffed
in a box
with three dead flies
oh!
and the tangled brush of a woman whom I loved

for one whole week
which
remembering her
makes me
lift my hand
as if to propose half a prayer
or to illustrate
the best way
to answer a deaf king

is to drop
a fist
on a heavy table
in place
of blasphemy's

last syllable
They take it
all

from a cold
rented
five-foot space
and
when I can't pay

they cross out my name
double- shackle

the gate
fill every
proper form
and price
the pitiful lot

for the block
They call me
to cough
up
over

and over
say: explain yourself: Shame
is like you're made
of 10,000
beautiful doors

and every day
you try to keep them
all
from flying open
at once
They reach inside
and take
the boxes of shoes
and old shirts
the third-hand
scratched up
oak desk
I heaved up
twenty steps
overlooking
West Grand Ave
With their battalion of metallic
hands
they'll take away
silence

They'll take away touch
They'll take music
too

which is when
I'll stand up
alone
and walk toward you
and offer a few fingers
for you
to lead me
to an empty floor
and sway
They'll take the light
They'll confiscate
my teeth
and leave
the knives with no handles

They take it
all away
They take away
weeping and
take away laughter
Not last to go
are the goats
as if

I could forget
the curses
And Ha-Haaaaa!!

they'll take
my eyes
and they won't even eat them!

They have taken
so much
I am standing
now

somewhere
at the end of a road
which leads to a beach
beside a sea
that a million ghosts
keep crossing

leaving everything
I once had
everything
I've become
everything electric
in a muscle
to make one
miniscule
move again toward

*The Beautiful*
in that wacky wandering
in that bloody
path
in that smoky
inventory
of a quarter century
in that ambling
in that sprint toward
every gorgeous
living thing
no matter
how tortured
or peaceful

I am going
I am almost completely gone
I am stepping away
Watch me

as I leave
the forks
I leave
the hammers

I leave
the bones
I am left
with love
I leave

the boiled coins
the thin shells
of swans
I am left

with love I leave
the latches and bolts
open
I am left again

and again
with love
I leave
and
I leave
and I am
left
again and again
and I can't seem to shake it
the rage leaves me
and leaves me
again and again
and love is left
it is all
that is ever

left
and today

I am blessed
I am the last thing
burning

SELECTED POEMS

Pause.
And begin again.
        —Kenneth Patchen

from
### *UPROCK HEADSPIN SCRAMBLE AND DIVE* (2003)

# B-Boy Infinitives

To suck until our lips turned blue
the last drops of cool juice
from a crumpled cup sopped
with spit the first Italian Ice of summer
To chase popsicle stick skiffs
along the curb skimming stormwater
from Woodbridge Ave. to Old Post Road
To be To B-boy To be boys who
snuck into a garden to pluck
a baseball from mud and shit
To hop that old man's fence before
he bust through his front door
with a lame-bull limp charge
and a fist the size of half a spade
To be To B-boy To lace shell-toe Adidas
To say Word to Kurtis Blow
To laugh the afternoons
someone's mama was so black
when she stepped out the car
the oil light went on
To count hairs sprouting
around our cocks To touch
ourselves To pick the half-smoked
True Blues from my father's ashtray
and cough the gray grit
into my hands To run
my tongue along the lips of a girl
with crooked teeth To be
To B-boy To be boys for the ten days
an 8-foot gash of cardboard lasts
after we dragged it
seven blocks then slapped it
on the cracked blacktop To spin
on our hands and backs To bruise
elbows wrists and hips To Bronx-Twist
Jersey version beside the mid-day traffic

To swipe To pop To lock freeze and
drop dimes on the hot pavement—
even if the girls stopped watching
and the street lamps lit buzzed all
night we danced like that
and no one called us home

# Freddie

Freddie claimed lineage from the tough
Boogie-Down Boricuas
who taught him how to break-
dance on beat: up-
rock headspin scramble and dive

We called it a suicide:
the front-flip B-boy move that landed you
back flat on the blacktop That
was Freddie's specialty—the way he'd jump
into a fetal curl mid-air then *thwap*
against the sidewalk—his body
laid out like the crucified
Jesus he knocked down
one afternoon in his mom's bedroom
looking for her extra purse
so both of us could shoot
asteroids and space invaders
until dusk
    That wasn't long before
Freddie disappeared
then returned one day as someone else's ghost
smoked-out on crack
singing *Puerto Rico Puerto Rico*
*las chicas de Puerto Rico*
That was the first summer we believed
you had to be good at something
so we stood around and watched
Freddie on the pavement—all day—
doing suicides
until he got it right

# Nine Thousand Outlines

If every story has its beginning
this one starts in the armpit of a god—the plots
of fishbone and vinegar a history of nails
a war or two a swan some saints of course some
slaves Eventually boys one day
toss bricks at a burst of starlings
then plash through the sky gathered
in potholes and oil-slick rainpuddles And
there is—that afternoon—a girl
awkward and pale crossing the lot
among scattered genuflections of sedans
and wagons The cooked rubber
fumes the projects when
those boys' necks erect and everything
sunstruck for a moment
become still

When I say I was once a boy who became
a wolf who became a crow who turned
to salt I mean I've become a man somehow
without remembering that girl: stork-
awkward and pale When I say
the boys are my friends I mean
all it takes is one of us startled
into quickness: a twitch
of the hip the others follow
and the girl—a contraption of wings—
stumbles for the nearest door

Some of you want to know
Some of you have already imagined
the short corridors the scramble up
each flight the landing where the girl cornered
raises her head once
to spit at the crotches crowded around
Do the boys drown themselves

or do they merely wet their snouts until
she becomes the river they want
Do you and I agree
these boys—when they're done—turn
grab their cocks (still hard)
then laughing emerge
into a parking lot now doused
in the dusk's chemical bloom

She'll still be there: slumped in a hallway
where I leave her so you can
cross the lot climb the stairs and see for yourself
It no longer smells like piss
It's a place where a girl can cower her whole life
where things have flung themselves
so far into the future time already reels backward
where twilight etches—in patinas
older than bone—9,000 outlines
of a girl whose endings I've traveled this far to forget
with all the lies a boy will work a lifetime to believe
until he's caught looking back

# You Clubhouse Boys

You Clubhouse Boys who
dance on the third knuckle
from the sun
         my heels burn
from the hell we help build
How many of us
         slit our hands
happy in the knife-glint scuffle
How many of us taste
the raw red rock
         in our chests
How many sing
         the *hilot's* song
spilled into New Brunswick streets
drunk with a borrowed liquor
we call time
         In this world
there is no act of contrition
and there is only
         this world
So I raise a glass to broken heads
and dead ones
         and new ones
born with fists
         to the murderers
and the murderers' grief
I raise a glass to blacktop drag
steeltoe thumb-toke
         I raise a glass
to side-sway
         I raise a glass
to the gun
         I raise a glass
to the metallic tang of blood
in the cheek
         I raise a glass

to the pipes and blacked-out windows
to back walls tagged up
                              torn down
to pulse-code bass
nightflash and deepthump ether
we sleep under like
                              crashing waves
I raise my glass to you:
who stumble this far
                              smoke scarred
fire stoked stoneblast
I raise a glass and count
                              how many
with dropped scabbed hands
are still left standing

*for CHP*

# The Next Hundred-Odd Half-Dreamed Miles

This part's real: the kid sways
near a curb (the club's fuck-hard
flash of neon lights keeps time
inside) his top lip split
mouth popped into hellglow blossom
eyes swelled shut like peaches
Small half-as-dark and twice
as yapping drunk as you
he swings forward and lands
a clean right cross you confuse
with a good reason to try
and toss him like a sack of trash
into the midnight traffic
His Pinay girlfriend (so light-skinned
and round-eyed she would have passed
for Magellan's daughter) shouts
*You goddamned monkey* in perfect English
which makes you hold
his head in your hands
—without thinking of his mother
cursing in Tagalog—
when you thrust one more time
the tender cartilage of his nose
against your knee except
this story isn't about you It's about me
and every time someone's bar-buzz
crescendos to mezzo-forte tough-guy
maybe I should consider that kid
holding both arms out as if he'd catch
whatever he could summon from the sky
but rage doesn't work like that
It's like this: I race down the Parkway
and skip every exit I know too well
slumped in the driver's seat
for the next hundred-odd half-dreamed miles
taking turns sucking my bloody knuckle

with the only girl I think I'll ever kiss
—my tongue too dumb to tell
which taste belongs to whom
and which mouth happens when

# Citrus City

When I walk down Second Avenue
                          the first
sun-spent day of spring
                          and the scent of dropped
flowers spilled bottles of OE and mints
begins to burn from the asphalt and people
strip to the waist reminded of some first urge
to be naked against the city air
                          (eight million breaths
at any given moment)
                          I see a boy devour
the last slice of an orange
                          and my mouth waters
so I buy one for myself
at the closest stand The citrus drips
down my wrists
                from the corners of my lips
and I realize it's been some time
                          since this joy: since
I've peeled and eaten an orange on the street
and it's been some time
                          since I've seen anyone
eat an orange outside
I look into the eyes of Manhattanites who
look me in the mouth
                and I think: perhaps she
tastes the same
tart under her tongue and maybe
she will head straight for a fruit stand and buy
a navel to eat on the street too
                          and someone
will see her or two people will see her love her skirt
sprayed with the minuscule burst of juice
so they buy lots of oranges
                          eat one on the bus heading
uptown (toward all those oranges

in the Bronx) and the person stepping off
at twenty-third walks crosstown to Chelsea
surrenders his organic nut bar
                    stops at a fruit stand
and maybe someone en route to Chinatown
bumps into the guy from Chelsea
and remembers his
                    first orange
                              at a picnic
as a child
              on a beach—
                    in the Philippines—
                              in August
So he buys two oranges
                    goes home to his lover
whose drape of sweat
                    smells like the day
and since he's already eaten one along the way
they sit across from each other
                    and share
the remaining one:
                    its packed flesh a brief but cool
reprieve from their apartment
                    steaming like an engine
and this is how a whole city's
                    eating oranges:
the first sun-spent spring day—
                    an orgy of them

# Who Says the Eye Loves Symmetry

Doesn't the eye love the ragged
tear of sky the treetop-shred
horizon The eye—after all—
loves the dizzy
dip of a road: its precarious
tilt towards a ravine
only wrist-deep water
and giant smooth rocks to break
the sky's fall The eye
loves the bit peach window agape
buildings caught mid-swagger across a skyline
The eye loves unpainted pickets
cracked planks the harlequin the prow
poked out of water
like a chin loves
the evergreen arched over a flood
like an old man looking into the street
for a hand loves a sawed link chewed
rope a birch's slants But
the eye can't
love what it can't
see: the woman
striding tired and brave amid the lobby's bustle
and under her shirt
a single breast

*For Maureen Clyne*

## "My Mother Is in Los Angeles"

Mom I wonder if dying to you
might be like landing
in Los Angeles on a clear day in March
still dressed for the Jersey winter
a little confused by a sky uncut
by factories and the Pulaski Skyway
a little stunned by pedestrians
who wait patiently at crosswalks
Are you intrigued by lemons from trees
—how for four days this city hasn't rained

I wonder if like me you ask yourself
why nearly everyone is so goddamned gorgeous
if you have to learn your way
around the wide boulevards
if you ever get used to people
who stare a little too long
when you ask for directions
or order a glass of water
And do strangers recognize your accent
then ask for news from the living
and do you have time
to visit the ones they bury

Mom maybe some things
vaguely remind us of home:
the rasp of a bad starter in the driveway
sit-com re-runs or a clip of Thurman Munson
blocking a fifty-nine foot change-up in the dirt
or maybe there's a house much like ours
where you held a Bible and rosary
praying to some dark ancestral sternum
where you learned about the rage of aging
in the arms of a god who answers
to ten thousand names
and none of them the one on your lips

This morning I stood on a pier in Venice
walked in a circle
a cigarette pinched
between my forefinger and thumb
When I looked out at the Pacific
for a moment I believed
I was stretched across the saltwater
For a moment I believed I was dead
suddenly thinking I was someone else
thinking I could fall madly in love
with this one and this one

I met a girl today who says she regrets
not seeing her sister the day she died
and I have nothing to tell her except
*My mother is in Los Angeles*
*and she manages to get around*

*For Liza Alegado*

# Uncommon Denominators

I add up the times I've fantasized about
women I've seen but never spoken to
and divide that by the hours
I drive past cemeteries and add again
the weight of breath in your mouth
measured in the ancient Tagalog word for *yes*
—but the number always comes out the same

So I subtract the moon
and the smell of incense on Good Friday
trying to connect Planck's Constant
to the quantum moment between
a candlelit flick and the back of your neck
setting aside my 7 dreams of having sex once
with Tyra Banks who tells me *God*
*You Filipino guys know*
*how to make love to a woman*
and even if I tally the 10,069
channels launched by satellites
which have an asymptotic relationship
to the count of stones cast
from a sinner's fist raised
to the power of eight million punch-clock
stiffs heading home late
still the number comes out the same
and when a beggar pirouettes
along an expressway's center lane
swearing this won't be his last
cigarette (smoke rising from
the rust in his moustache ) I suddenly know
the acceleration of a falling body
has little to do with slipping
a mother into the ground or
a whole greater than the sum of its parts

And if you ask what I'm doing
with 7 loaves and 4 fish multiplied
by the root of a dried tamarind tree
or the coefficient of friction
of a bullet on the brink of a rib
or the number of clips emptied
into an unarmed Guinean man
on a dark Bronx stoop I'll tell you
I'm looking for the exact
coordinates of falling in love plus or minus
the width of a single finger
lost along the axis of your lips

# Poem

*It takes a whole lotta sturdy faith hey.*
—June Jordan

Takes stones and a hole dug   deep Takes
a knot in the back and shoulders  slumped Takes
a whole lotta fallen
trees dead wood dry    brush Takes
genuflection at Black    Rock Takes
a psalm in the valley    blown Takes
a little sleep and one bad   dream
to wake up crying open my eyes
  and sing:     Damn—
enough stars up there to pin up
  the whole black   sky Takes
  one good     breeze Takes
a god with broad hands and a breast
soft enough for me to lay my  head To lay
  my head     takes
  prayer:
  *Thank you for dirt*
  *Thank you for stubborn oak roots*
  *Thank you for the trickle spring*
  *for the winged shadow circling*
  *without a name for sweat to cool me* *down* Takes
  earth and    lake Takes
  the night    Takes
  the stiff light by   moons Takes
fire to warm my feet and a dragon
  I can't     see Takes
a whole lotta faith—sturdy sturdy faith hey

# Pick-up Line Ending with a Prayer

When I tell la Colombiana I first met
a week before *Tu nombre*
*se queda conmigo* I know
this is a bad idea but
she doesn't stop me
with her stock stone stare
that sends away every other man
who's tried to speak to her tonight
I pull up my left sleeve
to show the sea and sun
tattooed on my forearm then
point and say her name
*Mar-i-sol* She smiles
I don't tell her the tattoo is a myth
of creation: a bird's trick to yoke
heavens and ocean in a titanic
barroom brawl: the ancient scrap
which has begotten all the continents
of desire: even the four-foot liquor-stained
ellipsis where Marisol and I will stand
at the corner of a crowded New Jersey dance floor
some 500 millenia later

I need to know something
about the legacy of beauty she inherits
the way a coastline inherits salt
I have yet to learn the catalog of unloved
gestures a woman lets no one read
I have yet to understand grace
is not the absence of awkwardness

but an accumulation of so many
quirks the body finds a way
to make them happen all at once

Lord my job tonight is to fashion lies
as with any life-long ambition
I may not deserve to fall in love But
let this be true—the beginning
in which there was only an ocean and a star
and a little pain we called distance
Let there be a bird with nowhere to alight
who taunts the heavens to water
who riles waters to the heavens
Let there be mar-y-sol Let there be land
and one day let it contain a dance floor There
let me recognize human grace when I see it:
every mis-step and slip
every foible and fuck-up
Let me know them
like the first errors of the sea

from
*MY AMERICAN KUNDIMAN* (2006)

# Meditations on the Eve of My Niece's Birth

Who sow buckshot glitter from Cape May to Arthur Kill
Who weave rush-hour Kyrie from lanes of masonry
and steel Who stammer boldface gospel on Newark
subway steam What rot feed one man Who record
his rasp Who transcribe his song Who unknot his
gut What spectral redshift beacons ancient
boogie-on-down What heats the heart's
enthalpic pith Who stop the clock—
submit to speed of light When
have I listened—child—How
will I begin When shall I
open my mouth
and let half
the world
fall in

*For Renata Mimi*

# On Our Long Road Trip Home I Don't Ask My Friend if He Thinks His Youngest Daughter Might Be Someone Else's Kid

The doe shudders a bit and the trucker
tells the woman who gored it with the front right bumper
of her late-model Chevy: *Your best bet next time*
*is to hit the gas and slam full force into the fucking thing*
Note to self: All things beyond logic are not
necessarily poetry The trucker draws his hunting knife
to slice clean the deer's jugular because he says
he can't take *it* anymore The *it* of his sentence
is probably as unclear to the trucker as it is to you
or to me or to Mikey who is telling me this story
on a ten-hour drive from the northern border
I like to think I'm doing my friend a favor by not mentioning
his two-year-old girl who laughs like him and shies away
from strangers just like her daddy does
though she looks nothing like him
and more like some handsome and nameless sucker
who invited Mikey's ex-wife out one night to wade naked
in the warm dark swamp of his crotch

I was about to make an argument for silence
and compare that silence to the trucker's knife
I was going to tell you it is a tool of mercy
and I was going to say quick sharp blades like that
are good for killing I could say all of that—but silence
isn't the knife and anyway I can't figure out
whose jugular to hack at or what suffering
creature I'd have to bloodlet first
or if we're simply better off slamming
full force into such gracile animals
Silence isn't Mikey or his dead mother
or the slut I make in my mind of Mikey's ex-wife
It is not even the vision of my own brother
lying down eyes closed on the Pulaski Skyway
inviting the fleet and heavy wheels of a sedan

over his fragile breast I'm thinking of that sudden
slender-bodied brute who rises from some
primitive and dreamless sleep and wanders
onto this boondock of an American interstate
staring into us late at night holding itself
steady before a two-ton rush of steel And still
my brother is not a deer and silence is not mercy
and I'm thinking of the mirth that trucker took
in finishing off a lame and bloodied mammal
and how neither Mikey nor I have the stomach
for the best of that sort of kindness which is to say
we are saving each other from the truth
and I'm doing my part when I jam the gas to the floor
headlong into the dull unlit road toward
the Jersey neighborhood neither of us wants to go back to
ready to make venison of the first swift beast
that dares to cross our path

# Beast

They call him Beast where he's from and he will tell you
that each living physical moment *affords an opportunity
to do something unique and beautiful* Now clearly this is
bullshit You see I first became acquainted with Beast's
grunt-and-howl metaphysics at a dust-sucking
half-court game every Wednesday night in grad school when
on several occasions—yes—I stripped the ball from him
clean *Beautiful?* No—It was *ugly* And in the tradition
of the many monsters who came before him he did not cry
for such ugliness This Beast is six-foot-four and speaks
five versions of Pound-And-Pummel In South Philly
I'm watching him play summer league where Beast thinks
he's a poet even when he hauls down a brick
off the defensive boards and there's four other
black men on the court calling to him
*Beast! Beast! Beast!* He answers them
with all the sensitivity of a cretic foot: a quick
pivot mid-court that knocks the opponent's skinny
two-guard off the gawky pair of iron
skillets grown out of the poor kid's ankles and projects him
like an old neurosis across the crud-ridden gym floor
More than once I've caught Beast's blunt left wing-
blade of his broad back on my chin And then with my best
blacktop ineloquence cursed him: *Thank you Fuck you too*
Isn't this so often the affection between men
that we should share not a single lovely word unless
through a battered mandible This is how I listened to Beast
recite after those Wednesday nights his invented
names for fire in such holy brag and trash but also how
one morning over tea in a more muted bravado
he narrated the quiet trauma of his father's final weeks how
his old man—whose oak-switch cruelty Beast had long
survived—was shrunken down to a pair of scrawny wrists
How they yanked at the tethers to the gurney
with whatever will he could scrape from his gut
already nearing the end of its slow-cook to soup

Beast's father—conjuring one last good ass-whooping glare –
would shake his head pointing to his own mouth
He was signaling his son to remove the ventilator tube
shoved a full foot down his rotting neck Every nerve
in his failing body yowling soundlessly *No Not*
*this I don't want this Take the goddamn thing out* And Beast
dutifully answered the way any noble animal
must answer its closest kin: with his body With the dangerous
radius of his shoulders With his muscled trunk And with his breath
He watched the last of his father's silent wide-eyed squawks
and enacted a son's most loving disobedience
He held himself—for hours there—perfectly still

# Lapu Lapu's Envoy Conveys His Response to Magellan

*"The teachings of history show that to send a score or so of*
*Europeans in coats of mail against a thousand naked slaves,*
*Indians, or what not, armed with fish-bone lances, was by no*
*means absurd . . . A few gunshots, a few shrewd blows, and*
*Silapulapu's poor fellows would be on the run like hares."*
—*Conqueror of the Seas: The Story of Magellan*, Stefan Zweig

Anger—you sonofabitch—is but one god and gods require
men to pray: to hold in their lungs some old nameless ghost and
    distend
their puny human chests with it 'til they damn near break then merely
    bend
down as if their backs have been whacked raw with rattan before
    their own pyre

What do you know of the twenty-one tempests we can conjure
with a kiss How our saints bless our barbs with venom  How we'll deify
your scrawny handsome messiah (He will love us too will teach us to
    defy
you who rattle the blue belly of heaven) If not with power

then with craft and ken will we coax you to our shores kill you and
    plant
—beside the stained brackish waters—your pale spear-pocked remains
And the god of salt who is the god of love and labor will mend
my brave soldiers' blood with your own Traitor . . . Christian . . .
    sycophant

May this god of anger  who is the god of fear with both eyes closed give
me the wits to release him quickly May he grant me the grace to
    disbelieve

# When You Haven't Made Love in a Long Time

Whatever first summons back her mouth
to yours—gin or lies or the massive electric
wreck of an old man's heart Whatever rouses
your clumsy pulse to its blessed hectic

measures Whatever lusty villain's
vague halo or blissless wrist you mimic
Whatever thoracic harbor your passions thrill in
Whatever ash and lye Whatever fragrant muck

lets your tongue be neither simple nor mad-dash
without knowing first the ramshackle
angles of angels rising Do not rush
from *if* to *yes* Travel a gentle sickle

Climb her thigh's solfeggio Hush along her hips like
some cool crooning devil eager to lose his wits

# The Woman You Love Cuts Apples For You

and stirs them in sea salt and vinegar
She takes a drag from her Silk Cut

eases again through the fruit's flesh
the blade stopping short of her thumb

You are both sweating at the shoulder
(East Ham's hottest summer) And you realize

these are not the times to come to poetry
You have everything you need

Your father's bone-hard stare
can't reach across the Atlantic

so you save yourself for another day
because there is this woman slicing apples

stirring them in vinegar reminding you
of an afternoon twenty-five years ago when

you knelt with your brothers at your mother's
feet to pluck apple slices from a small basin

pinched between her legs And one of you
would lift that bowl—almost completely empty

except for a sour clouded liquid
and a few seeds shifting at the bottom

You'd just taste at first but soon you're handing it
from brother to brother gulping lung-fulls

of that tart cider You'd sweat sniffle gasp chug
'til your lips turned white and numb

And before you went out into those Jersey streets
you'd rinse your chin You'd soap your hands

because the girls would hold their breath
for every reason and stink on your fingers and neck

You won't dare tell anyone you've learned
to love the taste of something so strange until this

woman cuts apples for you in vinegar
and the familiar fumes fill your nostrils and gullet

She will lift the bowl to drink She'll twist her face
and laugh when she offers it and you will drink

and she will drink and you will drink again
She will kiss your cut knuckle She'll kiss your eyes

Of course the vinegar stings
It's the hottest summer ever in London

And you and the woman you love fall asleep side by side
like this—reeking and unwashed—breathing in

each other s dreams of open skin

# Kundiman In Medias Res

and I like sometimes to begin
in the middle of things
your breastbone/navel
the small of your back
your hand's syntax pausing
at the comma of my thumb
I love your 700 questions
each strand curled long
across my lips the sudden
punctuation of your spine
Your mouth an interrogative
sliding from unknown
to unknown They say
one sign leads to another
I say each tastes vaguely
like blood Along my body's
broken lines I am still unwritten
by your fingers' calligraphy

Love—decipher me
Speak me with your first tongue

# Kundiman on a Dance Floor Called Guernica

*Don't push me 'coz I'm close to the edge*
*I'm tryin' not to lose my head uh huh huh huh huh*
                    —Ed Fletcher (a.k.a. Duke Bootee)

This woman and I are watching the b-
boys contort cocksure

swagger into dance Down
to the very ligament their bodies

are wattage their names writ in whiskey
and smoke their legs scribble

into the room's boned twilight
a gospel according to Duke

These dancers are thunder's bastards
And at the borders of their human maelstrom

a woman's hips are winding their own
slow vortex between my hands

We twist time with our waists
Each sweat-slick bass note hangs

in the room like a heavy bruise
healing its way to another storm

I am losing my hands to her
I am learning to drown

above water
But make no mistake

We think we are not in love
And no one can hear us

We are moaning for each other's air

# Kundiman Ending on a Theme from T La Rock

Your morning's
everyday stained
caul of exhaust Your
plum bludgeoned
dusk Your fine
stench and luck-
less French kiss
Your can-I-get-
down bliss Your god-
gone blessèd
Jones for loam
Your Jersey baroque
Your Mercy
9's sirens prying
every sky Your
name Your flow
Your funk Your every-
day nasty Your very
revelry Your break-
neck scat the loot
you boost Your
rags Your seven-
thousand-island
slang Your hype
Your hips Your spit
Your sickest wit
and snip Your every
severed syl-
lable Your blunt-
toke fables Your
smoke's reprieve
Your lever's
torque bearing your
body every
day Every lovely
mucking hum

Your mic sound
nice Every Check
One Your
fade Your cut
Your Knife Your
jazz on-two Your bass
Your every clef Your
left breast Your
folly Your lung
Your modest rot
Your alibata
tongue Do you want it
(*Hell yeah!*) Baby –
'cause it's yours

# Kundiman for My Lover Beside Me on the Floor
# (Her Daughter Asleep on My Bed)

There are things I would like to know
right now: a woman's left hip called morning
her right hip called night
and the secret blossom between
slowly becoming dusk
how long to hold the anaphora of breath
along her sternum  Every day I say
*Tell me what you like* and every day you say
it's your daughter's fingers twirled in your hair
Once it was the calluses of my hands
Tonight you sleep beside me
as though this is practice for the only way
you know to say goodbye

I've wanted to mistake your eyes for sadness
I've wanted  to kiss the wings
tattooed on the back of your neck
to know your belly by its quiver I've wanted
to touch your breast like a man
learning his name in Braille Maybe then
I thought I'd sleep for once without the dream
of being lost in the landscape of your lap
waiting for you to tell me where I am
as if I could find my way back
as if I had some idea of home
as if I could ever live
where my heart was not ashamed to break

# Poem for My Extra Nipple

Burnt-out sun shut eye
still-born amoeba
miniscule miscarriage
of the flesh ant head
desiccated heart
a volcano's embryo
unborn twin budged
through my breast misplaced
knuckle I let my woman
kiss me here: this
brown pearl of Olongopo
Bay thorn pierced
inch-deep into dermis
milkless gland
the aria's last note
lost between armpit
and sternum It is a secret
passage to the aortic
contortions behind my ribs
swollen sand grain
from the beach where
I watched my brother
nearly drown
– I pray to it –
the singed hint
of some great-great
grandfather's sin
come back

# About the White Boys Who Drove By a Second Time to Throw a Bucket of Water on Me

*"... there shall never be rest*
*'til the last moon droop and the last tide fail ... "*
—Arthur Symons

The first time they merely spat on me and drove off
       I stood there a while staring down the road
    after them as if I were looking for myself
         I even shouted my own name
But when they cruised past again
       to toss a full bucket of water
    (and who knows what else) on me
         I charged—sopping wet—after their car

and though they were quickly gone I kept
      running Maybe it was hot that August afternoon
    but I ran the whole length of Main Street past
the five-and-dime where I stole Spaldeens
         and rabbits' feet past the Raritan bus depot
      and Bo's Den and the projects where Derek and them
    scared the shit out of that girl I pumped
         the thin pistons of my legs all the way home

Let's get real: It's been twenty-five years
      and I haven't stopped chasing them
    through those side streets in Metuchen
         each pickup b-ball game every
swanky mid-town bar I've looked for them
      in every white voice that slurred and cursed me
    within earshot in every pink and pretty
         body whose lights I wanted to punch out

—and did To be honest I looked for them
      in every set of thin lips I schemed to kiss
    and this is how my impossible fury
         rose: like stone in water I ran
all seven miles home that day and I've been

running ever since arriving finally
here and goddammit I'm gonna set things straight

The moment they drove by laughing
at a slant-eyed yellowback gook
they must have seen a boy
who would never become a man We could say
they were dead wrong but instead let's say
this: Their fathers gave them their rage
as my father gave me mine

and from that summer day on we managed
to savor every bloody thing
that belonged to us It was a meal
constantly replenished—a rich
bitterness we've learned to live on for so long
we forget how—like brothers—
we put the first bite in one another's mouths

# As Glass

When these sons of Buenos Aires holler
in chorus from the muck-blessed soccer field

across the street they are calling to me
in the formal idioms their fathers use

to ignore the ubiquitous feral dogs
and the beggars of Recoleta

I understand just enough to fling
back halfway to the park's paved border

their summer-toughened leather ball
and return to my hardfloor Palermo flat

to phone my dad back in Jersey: *Papa* I say
*Tu hijo habla* Of course at first he doesn't

recognize my voice or even his own name
for I am speaking to him with an affection

whose prepositions point in all the wrong directions
but for six full minutes we are unfamiliar

with one another's rage For once
we are laughing at the same time

It's simple: we don't loathe one another in Spanish
like we do in English—a language I've long known

for its fluid burn The way it rises from my father's
ankles into his belly from his torso into his limbs

like molten glass This is why he and I
can glare at one another for decades

without moving—all the lexicons
of sadness and delight turning cold and hard

about every muscle and bone twisting
around the capillaries flooding the metacarpal nooks

stopping in the esophagus So if flesh sinew and gut
(this human crucible) were to fall away—as it must—

what's left is the clear anatomy of a man
cast in language unsummoned for 77 years

the whittled wooden fans of his childhood
his mother's kalesa rocking over Vigan cobblestone

a whore's warm breasts flushed against him
like a good bottle of rum cracked cathedral windows

some cots and soup and all 400 years of horse shit
poured hot through his veins and I

am there too—sitting in a chilly apartment in Palermo
listening to the fading howls from the football field

the bold charity of a foreign tongue sweetening
the image in my mind of this quickly aging man who

whacked me and my brothers silly with his leather belt
And down the street I can still hear those boys

teasing one another in lunfardo Maybe they're not too young
to despise their fathers Maybe they can already taste

in the prayers they pretend to say before they sleep
that petty venom distilling in their mouths But not today

Not in this Castillian For today this speech
of imperial thieves this dialect of conquerors this

larcenists' parlance I am taking back
as my own and every word of every tenderness

I have failed to speak is already rising through my knees
as glass It is ancient and it is pure It is not free

of bitterness or grief  It is heating
my very fingers as I write this: I want to learn

to love more fluently even if it means in English
I should shatter into the body of my father

# St. Patrick

After the man
they say chased
the snakes
out of Ireland
after the patron of the day
my father was ordained
into the Church
he wanted me
baptized
with a word
clicked shut
like a trap My name
starts with the brittle
snap of kiln-
dried wood and ends
with a trick It claims
my skin my flat
nose thick lips
the eleven ways
I've kissed one
woman to sleep

When I die
I want my friends
to christen me again
dab my head
with oil bless
my lips with rum
I want them to give me
a name they'll tag
in alleys chisel
into rock cracked
in its side
a name as far
from heaven as the next
George Street bar

I want a name like
a Luther Vandross
slow jam like
a kundiman like
a New Orleans doubletime
march something
they can pour
on the floor
stomp on
with their shoes
grinding it
to dust I want them
to dance
till their god-
forsaken feet
turn blue

# Two Black People and a Filipino Near the Concessions Stand at the Geraldine R. Dodge Poetry Festival

It wasn't bad the man held back your fries
and asked if you'd already paid It wasn't bad
me you and Nic had just enough money
to get us home trying to buy for the three of us
one large lemonade (no ice with two extra cups)
And it wasn't bad a drink cost one
half of what each of us had that day and 1/10
of everything we owned No—we conferred beside
the food stand about our lack of bank when
a woman in an Eddie Bauer vest asked
*Are you on line* You shook your head *No*
And she said: *Thank God I didn't want
to be killed or anything*
                                How long the pause
before we realized we didn't all hear
the same thing wrong How long then before
the three of us bust into laughter from
disbelief almost fallen forward
rolling in Jersey dirt till our guts knotted like
a Ha-Ha-Oh-Shit-God-damn giddy rot let loose
in our bellies How long Dunny

The next time some motherfucker asks if
you already paid you can tell him *Over
and over for 400 years* You can tell him
you got a wife and four kids and you write
poems Matter of fact you can tell him *Man
give me that side of fries two cokes
 for my friends plus forty-one
acres and a mule*

For Asheba, Nicole, and Carleton

# Photo of My Grandmother Running Toward Us on a Beach in Ilokos

Consider how happy she is
carrying the whole load of an ocean

on her head the way some women carry
water or fruits or fish My Lola

and the whole goddamned ocean
Tides Whalebone Reef And my dark

dark cousins stomping through the breakers
She is closing her eyes running

toward her American grandchildren
who wait for her on the shore

She is sopping wet trying to balance
an entire sea on her head Her arms are

flung wide open And she laughs
as if she were asking us

to bring our burdens too

from
*BONESHEPHERDS* (2011)

# Boneshepherds' Lament

A boy who played Chopin for my parents one afternoon
led another boy to the woods and hacked him in the neck
forty-two times with a knife
hoping squirrels would run off with the skull.
He and his buddy went back with slip joint pliers
to twist and yank, but they couldn't pull out the teeth.

When the fat-fisted teachers of my childhood spoke,
they told us the soul's ushered finally
to some bright space beyond a grand entry
where anonymity is a kind of wealth.
The sentinels, they said, are neither benevolent
nor cruel, though, as a fee, they take your name
in exchange for spending all of eternity looking at God.

So I aspired to be nameless and eternal
until the day I got enough balls to tell
those nuns and brothers in baggy cassocks
to go to hell, and in doing so, I was really committing them
to perpetual memory, the inferno being a place
where one's name is never forgotten.

But let me begin again.
                In the barrios of Ilocos Norte
there are precisely two words for slaughter.
In some languages, there is only one word for the sound of the tides'
trillion dice set loose on shores. In other languages
it's the sound of smashing chandeliers. My parents were born
on an archipelago where people worship salvation and ruin,
where, even if you can't see the waves,
you can keep the sound of shattering glass to either side of you
in order to keep from being completely lost,
                      though sometimes
you can wake up half way around the world
in the middle of the night, in a barrio of Ilocos Norte where
an infant crying is really a 200-pound sow

bound to a spit hoisted onto the shoulders
of two men in jeans and flip flops who deliver
the pig howling all the way from pen to block.
The men, then, laughing, slay, bloodlet, and gut the hog,
which gurgles, which is the same sound, my cousins say,
that is pressed from a man's chest
during one drunken night of bad karaoke
when he is stabbed five times through the armpit
until he's leaking like a bad jar.

It's true. You can ask a dead man's son, watch him
sweep the masonry floor to his father's crypt,
as he buffs their tiles into the kind of deep
blue that fills up small, unlit rooms by the sea
just before a typhoon starts swinging
its massive hammers down.
You might never get a second chance
to interrogate the accomplice, so ask him too,
and you'll know the accomplice is telling you the truth
if he hands you by the neck that dead man's only guitar,
all the bone inlay pried off, the body painted blue.
I know who killed his father. I'll never say.

My friends, have you ever taken a gun
out of the hands of a murderer
                                        as a gift,
just to shoot a few live rounds into some slapdash target
fashioned from calabash and deadwood?
And in return do your ancestors expect you
to simply shutup and bring to the murderer a bottle of rum
and—god help you—a song?
I don't remember much about the Chopin that one boy played
or much about the other boy he killed, except
he had brown hair and was the only white kid on the field
during our pick-up football games.
I remember the summer he went missing,

I stopped going to mass. And then I fell in love
with a girl as faithless as me, how she could sing
the devil into a Jersey cathedral choir.

Sometimes I dream of a city inside me, specifically
the edge of one, where a few low-wage grunts marshal
through hip-deep waters of a flooded street
a flock of bobbing carnage, bloated to sea-deep proportions of pink.
No one in the dream asks where they've come from.
No one mentions where they're headed, and the workers,
they're too exhausted by shift's end
for more than a crude joke or a six-pack
and a half-hour of Chopin on public radio.
I once stood twice that time in front of a single Goya painting
in which soldier and civilian alike face off, point-
blank in a skirmish. Their eyes wide and juvenile, the tender
yowl of their faces, their soft bodies rallied to battle,
they shoot and slash one another down. They seem boys
of snarling matter. They are men, women too,
darkened under the sky's forty-day gray.
In the far background, on a hill, a single figure of ash
appears to raise both hands, the human pose of victory
and surrender, and maybe what Goya wants us to see
from this distance aren't arms flung up—but wings: an angel
waiting to transport the grave bodies off the battlefield,
over the bright hill where he stands,
where no one will see them in good light.

# Delenda Undone

*after Cornelius Eady*

And so we've all been told to shutup (*Don't talk*, they say,
*too fast, too loud, or for too long. Don't take too much time
trying to tell the truth*). But this is my work, to break out
among strangers into laughter, how I've watched
small children, for example, fill with the lucky gust
a poem can ride into the near stillness of a room
and dance. For that, I am always, as now, grateful.

My father tells me, in his seminary days,
during the Japanese occupation,
most of the priests who ran that school were German.
The boys, then, were to speak only in Latin,
and would surely be slapped three Sundays back
if heard speaking the language of my father's country,
which is a beautiful country and a beautiful language,
and which has a curious word for being
so suddenly seized by affection, you clench
every muscle from your eyelids to your toes
for wanting to hold a loved one tight, to squeeze one
and kiss one so deep, you place yourself and your beloved
on the brink of physical harm. There's no word for this
in English, no word for those small provinces of silence
or for the kind of love that will trouble that silence
into music. My work is trying to find the very word
rippling in my body, which is a woman's body,
my mother's, and a man's body, my father's,
and nowhere to be found in the languages
that have conquered the lands my ancestors.

On the outskirts of every empire, there are man-made
lakes large enough to receive with ease
one hundred villages' worth of bones tossed into them.
This is a fact: there are more than seven million Ilocanos
in the Philippines, maybe a million in diaspora. All of us,
at one time or another, have been told to shutup, don't talk

too loud, too slow, or for too long, in Saudi
Arabia, in Madrid, in Tokyo, in Milan, on Bowery
near the foot of 1ˢᵗ Street. We've been told this. Some of us
have been famous liars, Ferdinand, for example
(who married another liar, Imelda), and my grandfather,
kapitan of the barrio, who claimed to kick the shit
bare-fisted and single-handedly out of fourteen ruffians
in the small barangay of Santo Tomás. Actually,
he kicked the shit out of five—nine ran away. These are not
lies. This is the truth. I'm not wealthy. I can't buy
space or time on billboards or websites. The name I inherit
doesn't part columns in the city's Daily Journal.
My family comes from a long line of farmers.
My cousins scrub their chopping blocks with salt.
They shush the goats before they kill them.

# Little Men with Fast Hands

The sweat flicks from your elbows
when you deliver the sweet no-look
to the big man on the wing. You've been running
whole crews since noon. It's a hard country,
ninety feet long and fifty feet wide, and
everyone on the borders wants in. And no one
belongs for more than forty-eight minutes
at a time. You know most all the players' names,
some you named yourself. You know,
in a half-court set, how to pick a crossover
from a point guard's hip
and when to talk shit to the seven-footer
who dunked on you last week—hard.
They know you'll chase down
the lead man on a fast break
and eat gravel just to make sure
the young gun with the swift first-step
is the only one not smiling when the two of you
square off next time. You know how to box out
a stocky forward on the inside with a slick
hip-pull so the ref can't see. You are
a little man with fast hands,
come from a long line of stealth
and flash like the Filipino scout who scaled
solo the sheer face of a mountain
with nothing but a bolo blade in his teeth
to reach a small squad of slumbering Japanese soldiers
in a cave camped out. The scout slit the necks
of fourteen without waking them. He let the fifteenth
sleep. This is just ball, but you know what's up.
Our hands are quick. The history's deep.

# Bienvenida: Santo Tomás

*For Uncle Charlie*

In the middle of my uncle's yard.
a goat, bound at the hooves,
wags its tongue.
I've traveled 10,000 miles
to be welcomed home
by a town that knows me
only by my middle name
and photos sent by post
more than twenty-five years ago.

And there is an old man
from the foothills
of the barrio's far edge
who has heard my Uncle Charlie
drag this small beast to the block,
heard the news by music,
the bottles, the banging, the laughter
inside the slaughter.
The old man limps
the half mile by foot
up the long dirt road,
unshod, a ratty tank-top,
a brand new Vegas cap,
a cut black strip
of inner tube draped
around his neck,
and in front of him, he is
rolling, the whole way,
a common jug on its side,
emptied of all its vinegar,
dusty, immense,
to his hip in height
and three times
the old man's girth.
My uncle is strumming the guts

out of his ukelele
when the old man arrives
and sets the huge jug upright,
pulls the bike tube
off his nape and stretches it
across the jar's massive
ceramic yawn, holding
the rubber strip in place
with one big muddy toe,
and on the downbeat
of the first measure
of the second chorus
he joins my uncle
in the kind of mooing
—these beloved geezers
swear—has several times tricked
a field of blossoms
into bloom, the old man
plucking from the makeshift
bass, not so much a moan,
but a pulse that ranges
a full octave
into each man's chest,
the sinews of the old timer's arm,
straining, the long muscle
of his back, taut,
his quadricep, his calves,
his black foot pumping
blood into his whole
awful body, his maw
flashing every one of his seven
good teeth to heaven,

and if a man become
the heart of a giant, the song
of a giant, each one of us

laughing like a giant,
if each one of us fulfill
the exact measure of a man,
and if the goat, at the same time,
is singing as it's dying
among men who are singing
and dying, the youngest
cousin among us, butcher,
slaughterer, elbow deep
in the animal's belly,
does not sing,
the carcass, bloodlet
now, also silent,
as if its stillness
were a source of music too.
The way, in death, one becomes
all the sounds one cannot make—
The sum total of everything
the living cannot say. Sometimes
we have to sing just to figure out
what we cannot say.

# Tamarind

This morning, my cousin Joseph and I both stink
from drinking too much the night before,
pumping into a karaoke machine enough coins
to make wages for one family's
week and a half of work. In this country,
you don't have to walk too far or listen too hard
to hear such miserable hymns. Ten years
out of jail, Joseph has hands like twisted copper.
He can go weeks without a razor to his face,
tells me he half-embraced the man he killed
by cudgel during a drunken scuffle.
Today, it's our job to fill a couple buckets
with a few kilos of sour fruit we'll soak in vinegar,
a remedy, our uncles teach us,
to douse the thousand rum-sick
monkeys howling between our ears. Lucky
it's October, when one good rain can detonate,
from the smallest sprigs of the oldest tree
on my uncle's farm, hundreds of swelled-up
tamarinds overnight, and those limbs,
weighed down, will sag so low their tips
will graze our thighs, half a year's worth of light
stewed until a whole tree's acidic nectar
turns to a sticky, thick bounty of fat husks.
Even hung over, we can't contain ourselves,
hoarding, with one hand, two and three tamarinds
at a time. Joseph is humming some version
of Sinatra when I drop my bucket to snatch
one fruit twice the bulk of a big man's forefinger
bulging off its branch, but the pod (which I barely
pinch with three fingertips) bursts
to dusty fog and a couple brown flakes
clinging to the ruined fruit's few limp veins.
What's more, the busted husk has unfurled
a fine line of burgundy around my hand and wrist.
Turns out, a mass of ants has hollowed out

the tamarind and left its dry, fragile husk
intact, until I crush it open and set loose a delicate
rivulet of dark red running up my trigger finger and thumb,
swarming now my wrist, splintering several swift paths
around my elbow, a thin sleeve of fire writhing
around my forearm. I stomp both feet hard
to shake the critters free. Joseph, by now, has lost his mind,
laughing, and I've lost all good sense too. I'm still brushing
the last dozen little beasts from my armpit
when Joseph takes my hands in his and claps them,
as if that could make them clean. Today, I'm grateful
to dance beneath a tamarind tree
beside a two-bit assassin instead of the woman I adore.
We will spill the tamarinds across a table
and our aunts and uncles will break from work
to join Joseph and me as we peel the fruit one by one,
lick the drippings from between our fingers. We taste
sap and salt in our own skin's grit. We suck the fruits'
sour green pulp down to their smooth, ruby-hard pits,
these seeds in our mouths click against our teeth
before we spit them out and rattle them in our palms
—like so many muddy gems and so many bloody stones.

# Crew Love Elegy

On October 31, 1984, I hopped into a Datsun
with three other boys and cruised
the neighborhood next to the Country Club
just to see what the rich kids dressed like on Halloween.
No one believed I'd jump out the car window
and press the point of a dull, four-inch blade
against that chubby kid's belly and tell him
*Hand over the bag.* I was a good Catholic boy;
I wanted to convert the disbelievers. So my threat to cut
that kid down was quick: I flashed a five-dollar balisong
and my best altar-boy smile. I don't care
what you say. New Jersey is beautiful at dusk. In winter
I love the insinuation of its cities through snow,
as if the white contours can't hold all our dangers down;
the stiff chimneys sear into the sky a hole the size
of your hand, the portal, perhaps, through which heaven
snatches up small children or sends down vivid dreams
of butterfly knives and rich boys swinging bags
full of sweets. Come on. People go missing
all the time. No one cries for them. Even if I give you
the neighborhood back, the country club, the rich fat kid
dressed like C3PO. Listen: I'll give you the whole bloody
New Jersey sky, that night, starless, magnificent. It don't matter,
because somewhere in the world I still brandish a knife,
though I go by another name, and with three of my friends
I've disappeared into the smoke of a banged up
Japanese import. I keep thinking if I just tell the story
again out loud, I could bring us all back to make things right,
but there's no trace, no knife, no stick-up kid or three boys
shamed into silence. I'm telling you, I hopped
into the Datsun and threw the bag of candy in the backseat
giggling. My friends said nothing. We were afraid of nothing—
for we were reared by a generation that could make
whole nations simply vanish. And like any good crew,
we kept waiting for an angel to come down through
a hole in heaven the size of a hand made in god's forsaken

image and shackle us to each other for good. It's no use.
You can retrace every inch of all the places I've ever been.
Trust me. I've looked. We're nowhere to be found.

# Sundiata Elegy

Sekou, only weeks after you died, I met a man named Elmond
at a resort in Puerto Plata. His job, to stand
at the commissary entrance every day
to make sure the guests had properly paid
and didn't show up naked for breakfast.
Elmond studied French history, wrote in Creole,
and every morning stepped into his beige company-issue
khakis to welcome as a sort of friendly sentry
the Dutch, the English, the well-to-do Americans.
He'd raised his several siblings himself, and sent each week
what money he could to his family in Port-au-Prince.
Every morning we chatted in Spanish
like two men met in common exile, quick
to open the doors of their inner laughter.

The afternoon we first talked, I offered him a book of poems,
which he took, not as a gift, but in barter.
I'd heard Elmond several times singing, strumming
a beat up steel-string and asked if I could perhaps take the guitar
just a couple days until I left, and would he hold this book
in the meantime as collateral, to which he twice said yes.
And for a day and a half, I was the one sonovabitch
on Hispaniola singing with my cracked voice
a full repertoire of corny ballads. At one point,
a man named Angel, who folded towels at the main pool,
came up to me on the beach, shushed me, and took the guitar away.
Then, as if to make further good on his name, he sang to me
*Quisiera ser un pez . . .* offering that ancient wish
with all the sweetness of flesh and honey. After,
he held the instrument at arm's length, gazing into it
as if he himself had cut and planed its wood.
Clearly, it wasn't so much the guitar he admired
but all the hands through which it had passed.
Angel began to name for me, not just Elmond, but every one
of a half dozen men working at the resort who shared the guitar—
busboy, custodian, bartender, musicians all of them:

Javier, Berto, Santiago, and Roqui, the blind masseuse
who claimed to hear things we could merely see,
each man keeping the guitar for some time, then
relinquishing it to the next man, until it was his turn
to hold it an hour or, as I had, a couple days at most
and Angel mused the guitar must have been older than
the oldest of all the workers, smuggled into lovers' bedrooms,
banged around in cramped buses and the backrooms of saloons.
Angel shoved the guitar back into my arms and told me to sing on.

The morning of my flight home, I found Elmond
at the entrance of the commissary reading to a woman
from the book I left him, which I told him to keep
as if our trade were even in the first place. He put it down
to make room for the guitar in his lap. I thanked him again
and shook each of his hands goodbye. As I walked off,
Elmond drew a chord across the strings, and the woman,
with her eyes still locked on him, sprang up, snapped
her chin over her shoulder and tipped her hips in rhythm
a few times, even her small collapse into laughter on beat
to Elmond's bachata croon. Sometimes I wonder
if music isn't just another version of light
slowed down enough for the living to dance with the living.

Brother, wherever you are, I like to think
you'll ask a pretty lady to dance with you tonight. If so,
I hope you'll listen for the distant music of borrowed guitars.
Surely, you've been waiting for news. So I'll tell you this:
it's cold in New York and raining hard, so that a million
strings right now shimmer through the alleys of your city.
You had a gift for hearing what the rest of us could only see.
You took up a whole nation's rage with two good hands
and heaved it above your head, hauled it down our boulevards,
bore it on your back through this adagio throb
of blue dream and steel . . . You turned it all into song.
I know this much. There is a man in Puerto Plata who can tell me

everything I need to know about the history of France
in a language his great grandfathers made up. I've come back
to live in someone else's house in the richest country
in the universe. None of us belongs anywhere
without love. Everything has begun to die.
Some of us keep shouting your name.

# Ars Poetica: After a Dog

> *. . . this baffling*
> *multi-people     extremes and variegations     their*
> *noise*
>
> —Robert Hayden

Here is a sex shop and a Bible shop
two doors down. Between them a sick hound roams.
Let's suppose this. There is also a two-
family house (where three families live)
across the street from a deli and this
check-cashing shack with a rabbit hutch out
back. Any of these may have been burned down
twice.
      Let's suppose this is America.

Over the years we have become the kind
of tribe that has forgotten how it trades,
over chess and chit-chat, a mango or
Jesus honey for knives. Now, we thank god
the almighty we don't know what it's like
to be close to one another. Georgy
the Idiot, for example, feeds this
sick dog flowers. And we watch him. But then

suppose two or twenty of us—more—
hear a sound, some familiar din, far-off
tambourines, children's laughter, though a bit
dark, like bell and bone, and it simply grows
until we are looking at each other
wide-eyed with this small thrill calling us out,
this handsome buzz-saw racket, this rhythm
that bores the air a gurdy hum. What if
our numbers suddenly flood a small stretch
of spoiled turnpike or dried out meadow, what
kind of sound is this that rallies us all
from precinct to nook, what noise to muster

tremors from King James and *Hustler* alike,
what uproar, what raucous fuss in every
American vicinity, and I
know you don't believe any human noise
can call us all together per se, but,

listen, suppose we *are* moved, summoned, you,
me, and the rest of us who want to know
something about everything we've outlived.
By hullaballoo, we gather, beckoned,
not too far from the XXX store and
the Bible store, not too far at all for
Georgy to carry in his sleeves the scent
of mongrel or bad cheese or onion skin
and cheap ink, and you and I and Georgy
and all stand, elbow to elbow, this small
throng of the ordinary, armed for once
with our *full* wits, and no, let us not say
it is a singing, but say this, this sound,
as we approach, gets stranger and stranger,
so much so, we mistake it for ourselves.
It has the bony rattle of dice-quick
wrists, the abundance of olives and lake-
shore sand. It resembles the scripture and
curse you and I, in dim-lit squares and dance-
floor muck, in crawfish mud and dancehall wine,
in broken-bed and graveyard bliss have been
grinding for all our lives, this joyful wind
and rewind of the body way back down
into jubilance so old no vector
of bullet or blade could fleck the soggy
pale neck of a boy offered to God, no
battalions of angels to save him, say,
what if this sound that is not a singing
becomes, one by one, the lot of us, us
improbable, us gorgeously common,

us tune's contagion. What if us do sing
with sand caught in our teeth, mango dripping
from our mouths. Jesus-honey wild, what if
the very knives start clanging too. What if
those first no-song strains open the sex-shop
neon in us, musk in us, whiskey stink
so deep down in us we sing like this: so
funky, so loud, we refuse to neglect
what ramshackle bunkhouse, penthouse, whorehouse
we were drawn from in the first place or how
the hell we will ever find our way back.

Even so, let's not forget, the long yawp
of the poor dog who ate fresh petals some
moron savant force-fed it, having spent
three full spring days stitching them together
with metal barbs,

              what if no one recalls
*that* sound,
        except
           the few surviving dogs,
the twisted thin-wire fence and the silent
magnolia blast every May. I say,
let us not slip back through the dark to sting
and peck our beloveds with more than our
usual misdeeds. I say, let us not
forget a sick hound's metallic hack and
skirl, for Georgy has found a few more dogs
to feed his barbed garlands to and before
we count ourselves among the blessed, let's say,
we ain't done yet howling into gray tombs,
ain't yet done cracking necks. Let's say this, once
and for all, for kicks, we won't taste sulfur
at the end of a fuse.
           When one is born,

when one dies, when one steals a moldy loaf
of bread—

       this is how it is. The dildos
go on sale, in the rabbit hutch a snake,
we've played checkers with all the pawns, but if
there have been any lies, we're sure to let
everyone know now what they are and who
started them.

        Some of us will not get fed
but let's listen, spooning in the dark, for
laughter,
      for if we're lucky, sometimes both
the darkness and the laughter are our own.

This is America. If we've no choice
but sing
      in multitude no better than
the soul of a wrongly punished dog, may
God, for once, not grant us many more things
as foolish as that, given the way we
ruin our guts on rusted steel and bloom.

# Naima

Mothers,
a sudden fog of honeysuckle
will guarantee you
no sadness
you can deny your children.

Let me tell you a story.

If you know how the A train gores
the dark with a steady hum,
perhaps you've come across
an old Caribbean man
patting his ass, his lapels,
first his front pockets
then again the back, looking
apparently, for a wad of bills.
He mumbles inward,

then reports to you,
*Three hundred dollars.*
*I had three hundred dollars.*
He looks you in the eye to assure you
he's known crueler losses,
and even though heaven likes to bore us,
a woman dressed in tattered
black makes her entrance
as the old Caribbean leaves, and

at the same time

a trio of gradeschool boys
(the first chaos of spring in them
about to erupt)
fling down
a canvas sack
foaming with fresh-cut honeysuckle.

They place, too,
on the subway car's floor
a radio. They bounce
on their toes

with a kind of pre-fight
jitter. The woman in black, in fact,
has a boxer's under-bite

and announces herself
like this: *Ladies and Gentleman, please*
*find it in your hearts to help a starving artist.*

So you can't blame the biggest boy
for slapping the middle boy
on the back of the neck
when the younger one reaches
for the radio's play button,
can't blame the older one
who sucks his teeth
at the younger one
as if to say: *Let her sing.*

By now,
you've almost completely forgotten
the Caribbean man,
when this woman eases out
her first, perfect, raspy sob;

there are only a few of us who don't
recognize the tune,

and since we think we can own
what's beautiful
by disdaining it,
we try to pretend we can't hear

the city's legacies of misery
trembling the tunnel walls.

How to explain you're watching
a stranger hobble by
and that you have to lift
your eyes twice
to make sure it isn't
someone you love?

I'm old enough now to understand
every silence is remarkable,
not least the silence of boys
swaying side by side

as a woman in black
walks the length of a train
with each crystalline note
poised in the air that trails her

and there isn't a scowl among us
when, behind her, the end-doors
gently smash,

signaling the boys
to blast the train with a backbeat,
then throw their bodies
down

in dance
as if to translate everything
we've lost today
into a joy
we can finally comprehend.

The boys shut off their radio,
gather their capful of dollars

and rabble of white blossoms

and pounce out at the next stop
in single file, but not—
I swear to you—

without unfurling
the first four notes
to Coltrane's gorgeous groan.

The subway doors close.

This is the end of the story.

We ascend one by one from the dark

and beneath us

Harlem's steady moan resumes.

# Aubade: The Monday Bargain

If only to be still                              If only an hour
If only our stank morning breath        If just to kiss your eyes
If just that and nothing more
If only the wicked hiss of wind to rattle the steel door in its jamb
If only the gentle stirring of gray water    If only its opaque twines
    spilling from my fingers
If only the history of ramparts and blockades If only the winter-dark
    of your skin
If only the history of skin and no more
If only to lie down in a room of vaulted dark sealed so tight you become
    the dream inside the skull of some ancient being or one not yet
    born among rows of cane and guns laid down for good
If only the smell of denim and sex If only to exile sadness and if only
    for now
If only the thick tendons of one burly husband's neck
If only blisters and bloody wood
If only the heart bulged by kick drum and bass
If only the names we craft from sadness
If only the names we scratch out And if only we shout instead
If only the children farewell If only their first curse If only their final
    sky come clear
If only one man to hear his dead wife's voice If only one to raise a
    goddamned good big glass of tequila and just one milagro to burn
    his throat back to baritone and raw silk
If only this and nothing less
If only poems like roaches crawling into the rooms of your childhood
    If only nothing to kill them
If only vast black mirrors cast far over the city at night
If only the gods we push up into them—their arms full of our best gifts
    If only a way for them to restore love where we've ruined it

Not here My sweetest name Not here in our bed in early morning
    where we wake slow to tell each other we've dreamed of things
    that cannot kill us that only fill us to our thumbs with laughter
If only laughter If only one brief burst of it If only the last monster to
    tumble out of my mouth

If only the stampeded garlands of dead kings If only empires and their
    engineers If only their serpentine mosaic paths If only the horses
    who shat freely on those paths marching
If only the garments of slaves only the seamstress of burlap only
    a chorus of secrets passed from mouth to mouth in a silo or
    boathouse or subway tunnel
If only that and nothing more than a wish to slip into the most mundane
    mysteries of the day
As if the day and the mystery of the day can only end at twilight
As if we couldn't right now open up our whole bodies
So that another century might begin

## Making Love to You the Night
## They Take Your Father to Prison

There's got to be

                a chorus

somewhere

              for the con-

junction

              of honey-

suckle

              and funk

a verse

              for the turn

of your hips

          and the slingback

steelbar

              anthem

banged-

           out breathless

over

              your father's

small-time

              under-

hand hustle

              a tune

that begins

            in the skin's

hi-hat

              quiver

begins

            with a lick

of the fist

                or the thrum

of a summer

                gust doubled

in the brief

                sweet

moan coaxed
from your mouth
and mine

                We grind

slow

                —two

bodies become

                one small

song scarcely

                loud enough

to budge God

                and any three

of his bloody

                saints

Baby

                we are our own

wine We

                improvise

the gorgeous

                toil

stillness

                and motion

against each

                other

make—bone

on blunt bone
gleefully
barbaric

Call it
blessed We
cull some-
thing like salt
out of the seep
of evening
air immense
and rising

like incense
so stink
hell-
fire must
work twice
as hard
to burn it
into us then
once again
back out

By dawn
you'll leave
my finger
between
your teeth

and behind it
the last grief
of the first man
you've ever adored

149

                              on the verge
of free


                              Sometimes
the body
                              in music
unlocks
                              its most ruthless
interrogatives
                              and to this
and the rest
                              of the world
tonight


                              I cannot

stop


                              saying yes

# Guitar

*For Shiela who wants to learn to play*

The bottom end's a little shallow
and you might need to shim the bridge
to hush the fifth-fret buzz. The action's low
and the neck, a tad warped, but I swear,
this thing sings. For ten years,
I've accompanied lovers, convicts, and children
with this guitar, bought it with my last
hundred bucks, fifty more perhaps
than it was worth that day.
I just wanted to touch nylon again,
to play the way my Uncle Eli used to,
'til cancer mugged him for his lungs. He sang, Sheila,
and the guitar did too. And that kind of singing
was like eleven acres of sky to a nine-year-old kid
terrified of a 50 mile-per-hour hard ball.
The summer my father came back
from burying his mother in the Philippines,
he told my brother and me the two oblong
boxes he pulled off the luggage conveyor
were ours. Once home, we pried the cardboard
apart, tearing the packing tape
and snapping the industrial staples
loose with our bare hands. I ran my fingers
slow around the slick soundhole edge.
I stuck my nose into the strings to smell
the jackfruit wood stewing inside
and when I pulled my face away,
the instrument made its first silken hum.
I don't know if you believe in time
the way I do, but when history touches us
it's like hearing a skinny uncle sing
with a cigarette dangling from his lips
without one note of misery in his dying,
and the guitar he's holding is yours.
You might not understand the words sailing

past you, but one day, years later, on a drive back
to Rockland maybe, where an old woman
scolded you as a child or kissed the small bones
of your shoulders, you may find yourself
singing, out of nowhere, that tune. I mean to say,
I never thanked my father for that first guitar.
I smashed it in a tantrum against my heel
and didn't own another until this one.
I should warn you, every guitar has its ghosts,
and they'll ask you whom you love and how much.
As for learning, your hands are going to ache
a little while, but one day, when the chords come easy,
the guitar will whisper to you some old secret.
Whisper back. The most beautiful intervals are ancient
and imperfect. They will teach you to love
something so deep, you will want
nothing better than to give it all away.

# Despedida Ardiente

*For Dale, Elizabeth, Stephen, J.D., Tori, and Cara*

Dear feverless, dear poets, dear love-
sick ones, now cured, there are
bloodless battles
to be won. Stout your maw
with your finest curses. Yap
your demons to their proper graves. O,
meek weepers! Asymmetries! Be
kissed! Let the trash stack
in the kitchen. Keep your lover
a full day from work. O, sweet
neglect! O, nectarine! Those
bitter pits are meant
for more than nibbling. There is
a holy jumpoff. There is a funky
genesis. There is
a reason love and jive
kind of rhyme. You oblong fruit
not three days ripe, somewhere in you
lies the science of typhoons, a dream
of strings. O, dirty word! O, first murder!
(O, cocoa butter whiff
on a smoky bus!)There are theories
we're made of mostly nothing
but motion. O,
gap-toothed guitar! O, soundhole!
You faraway drum. You slang-
mouthed blessing. You long
chime. You chamberless
sextet. Let me leave you
with a few last words: When
mad dogs break chains
to run at you, charge
back. Bare your very
teeth. No monster, I promise,
outruns you. Whack them on the ankle

with a stick. Chase the bastards
down. Listen—this vertigo, this
wreckage, this bad ballad
straining the thickest tendons of your legs—O,
darling sleepers, may you wake
in the middle of the night to strange
sounds. You champions
of laughter. All you have to do is speak
simply. Your business
is the truth. Your heart's
catastrophe is just
a little of history's
twisted bulwark.
If there weren't a sky
within your chest
worth breaking, believe
me, you
would have stopped
all this singing
by now.

# The Tradition of Pianos

*for Melissa Piano*

I've sat at spinets, toys, consoles and uprights,
banged through ballads, blues and pop on a Bösendorfer,
even jammed, drunk, in A-Minor on a concert grand
with Max Roach comping behind me. You know,
some pianos are beautiful by themselves
in the corner of a room with big light and a chandelier above,
but the sight of such an instrument is meant to draw you in,
its very silence an invitation. Its strings bear (did you know this?)
twenty tons of force to keep them taut,
so that just one meager human body bent to the keys
can shake a whole goddamned concert hall with—I'll say it—
love, the swelled tonnage of air becoming brisk, electric.
Old beat-up players, too, with their stinky scrolls
and sticky ivories, yellowed, they don't turn me back.
I like to touch them, to hear their honky-tonk shrill
like a voice famished into nothing but a thirst
for a shot of rum. And I don't mean one must suffer
in order to make Great Art, only that we all,
at one time or another, suffer terribly anyway,
so we have music. My sweet girl,

I wanted to write a poem about you, and all I could think of
was your name, all the stories asleep inside it,
the way a piano holds so many notes,
and each note itself, a choir, silent, until the choir's touched,
and my god, how whole crowds move when *they* move. I've seen it,
grand ballrooms bounding and body-rock basements
crowded with couples sweating muzzle-to-muzzle
to some playful son martillo swing. It happens.
Remember the night the Chelsea docks swayed beneath us, dancing,
and you clapped so hard and so long you broke your watch
and woke with both wrists bruised? We laughed at that. This—
this is what music can do, can let all the love out of us,
fearlessly, and we can boogie down—or kiss. I mean,
how many behemoths of loneliness have been tamed

with how little music? You don't know this, but
at the Blue Note, the night Amel Larrieux's daughter, Sky,
climbed onto that eight-foot Steinway and seemed to call up
from that box full of hammers every flawed song,
every reckoned sum of jubilance, rage and rapture, this
child, this mother and slender child, rejoicing
a whole bloodline's voice in toil. Rejoicing—
me, you. That night was the hundredth I imagined
kissing you along your shoulder. And the hundred first
I said nothing. Think, Melissa, of all the secrets between us,
and think of all the clandestine joys in the wood of one piano.
Consider the men who chop its spruce and maple down. Think
of whom those men must sometimes fail to love with all their might
when they go home battered and tired. Think of the truckers
who haul the wood for miles by rig to those quirky piano makers,
who conjure math and the devils of pig iron to engineer
some beast-scaled hunk, some apparatus that, played with both
precision and weight, falls only infinitesimally short of holy.
And think of all the unsaid bliss inside of you and me,
stored up for so many generations before us,
centuries of strange folk, with our same hands,
cuddling in the dark, hiding from each others' promises
of adoration. Go on. Close your eyes to me—but trust.
Art Tatum sought out pianos mostly out of tune
or whose keys didn't all work to test what good sound
he could coax from their partial ruin. What does it mean
that Lennie Tristano, son of Italian immigrants,
invented a style whose chords are lush harmonic clusters,
the wrists moving in close, parallel motion up and down
the keyboard? Who called that style locked hands? So Shearing
stole it, and Milt Buckner and Oscar Peterson perfected it?

I've known you these few years, but it seems I've been listening
to the history of pianos my whole life now. Bobby Timmons,
Phineas Newborn Jr., Monk—these are my heroes. And I know
Miles, for example, talked shit about McCoy,

but the summer of 1988, on the bedroom floor, I rigged a turntable
straight with no pre-amp and knelt to the speaker
with "My Favorite Things" playing over and over,
and I'd pop up to run between that hot, cramped wreck of a space
and the brown Baldwin in the living room,
until I finally doubled over on the stairs
and surrendered. I would never play like that.

If a piano can make a part-time, petty thug weep,
what will it do to a full-grown man with no better sense
than to profess his affections to a woman who reminds him
of all the gorgeous music that has filled him up for good?
All I know is there's a machine in the world
upon which I've placed my fingers countless times,
a contraption whose bulk is like god's one good fist,
which sometimes opens to reveal four centuries' worth of solitude.
If, one day, you and I should call each other *love*,
and you wake to find me in the next room,
leaned into the piano as though looking into a deep, living pond,
don't be scared to sit quietly beside me. I'm just listening,
as now, for the countless instances of touch,
lost in all the years of your name.

from
*BROOKLYN ANTEDILUVIAN* (2016)

# Despedida: Brooklyn to Philly

Out here, on the corner of Huntingdon and Trenton,
I can listen a long time to the skaters rail-slide
all June and July at the park, their boards igniting
tight fires against brick and cement, and the fruit lady's
apricots seem to bounce among the topless boxes
crammed into the bed of her pickup truck. This summer,
I said farewell to Brooklyn. I counted each river I crossed.
I know all the bridges by name. I don't owe my madness jack.
The bullhorn on the cab is blasting but it can't drown out
these grim whispers dogging me. In all the worlds I've loved,
I thought I could murder a monster if it had a body to drop,
a set of ribs to measure with a stiff jab and bury my best
left hook. But what about this outcast ache that trails me
like a thick fog of midges, this swarm of spectral pests without
legs or wings. Well, even a beast that can't be seen so easy,
even a creature freaky as Grief has a rhythm to catch. I've learned,
sometimes the only way to lay out a punk who ducks you
is to trick him into singing, a feat you can't achieve
unless you're willing to witness your own dazzling woe,
your maddening clangor. Then you've got to let it all go.
I'll be the first to admit, I've never been beautiful—
except when no one could see me, so beautiful
even I couldn't bear it. That's when I began to imagine
how to float from a silver maple or gather myself
in slow motion like one hundred eighty starlings
then simply burst apart again before the grill of a fast-
moving car. Later, I remembered how good DJs listen
to classic cuts we love on vinyl like a living pulse,
how the tempo's dragged and nudged in the rift
between snare and kick, each meter's kink and quirk,
a chasm that no plain magic can tap and no known math
can predict. The trouble's not a subtle one, to be
without a single nation or a home. And yet, ask
any veteran who has stepped away from his decks
to let them run untouched and he'll tell you: he has heard
the moment when two different tunes left to spin

at the same time line up, sync (sometimes for just
a single measure or less), before those downbeats
buzz loose again and stumble back into the gaps and breaks
of the other track, drifting into their double galaxy
of metal, wood, and space, clattering against one another,
simultaneous grooves, a pandemonium to hone your hearing,
—pickaxe and waxwing, hammer and flutter—the wind-up-
and-jump into the most gladdest double-step romp.
That's what great dancers learn to move to!,
the fickle swing of the meanest demons, the kind of juke
and rock that bears every burden—from cutlass to crib,
Brooklyn to Philly, bamboo to brass. So when the hellion
squads start their ghoulish murmurs, I summon
my every motley bell and nasty drum. I turn it loose.
That kind of thumping will make any ghost hum.

# Typhoon Poem

The teacher can't hear the children
over all this monsoon racket,
the zillion spoons whacking
the rusty roofs, the wicked tin streams
flipping full-grown bucks off their hooves.
Everywhere there used to be a river,
there's a bigger river now. Every hard face
on the block is sopping. Even the court
where girls from St. Ignominius ran
the roughneck boys off to play
their own three-on-three in plaid skirts
and church shoes for cash?—forget it.
The whole city's a flash flood
with brawn enough to flush trucks
sideways down the capitol's widest drives:
the crushed tonnage bobs around a bit
at the foot of some Spanish bastard's statue,
before it stalls and pools on white church steps.
Brute pilgrims. Face it, paddling dogs won't
make it, so children got no shot. But quick
thinking, the teacher lashes her students,
two at a time, with wire and stray twine.
She binds them across their breasts
to trees and metal posts lining the street's
half flooded walk. *No goddamned way,*
she swears. She won't let one little one
be washed out, even if their wriggling
makes their armpits bleed.
They'll have to make peace with the vision
of their uncles' and neighbors' blue
bodies bumping past before they fishtail
out of sight. You can't wish away
the deluge. You can't vanish
the bloated carnage-waters. But the tykes
in crew cuts and pigtails, still fastened
to shafts and trunks in ragged rows,

will survive. For now, their teacher
has made them safe by building an orchard
of them in the middle of a city road,
this small chorus of young hard fruit,
this little grove moaning.

# At the Tribunals

Once, in a brawl on Orchard I clocked a kid
with a ridgehand so hard I could feel

his top teeth give. His knees buckled
and my homeboy let loose a one-two

to finish the job. I turned around
to block a sucker punch that didn't come.

We ducked under the cops' bright red
hatchets that swung around the corner.

I never saw the first kid drop. He must
have been still falling when I dipped

from the scene and trotted toward
Delancey. He was falling when I stopped

to check my leather for scuff marks.
He was falling when I slipped inside

a dive to hide from a girl who got ghost
for books. He was falling when I kissed

the Santo Niño's white feet and Melanie's
left collarbone and the forehead

of one punk whose nose I busted
for nothing but squaring off with me,

his head snapped back to show his neck's
smooth pelt. Look away long enough

and a boy can fall for weeks—decades—
even as you get down on one knee

to pray the rotting kidneys in your mom's
gut don't turn too quick to stone.

I didn't stick around to watch
my own work. I didn't wait for

a single body to hit the pavement.
In those days, it was always spring

and I was mostly made of knives.
I rolled twenty-two deep, every

one of us lulled by a blade
though few of us knew the steel note

that chimed a full measure if you slid
the edge along a round to make it

keen. I'll tell those stiffs in frocks
to go ahead and count me among

the ones who made nothing good
with his bare hands. I'll confess,

I loved the wreckage: no matter
the country, no matter the machine.

# A Scavenger's Ode to the Turntable
## (aka a Note To Thomas Alva Edison)

We lifted the precious arm first, then the platter.
    We pulled free the belt, and unscrewed the top.

I didn't take shop or build a whole lot by hand,
    but I was pretty good with a knife. I poked the half-

dull blade clean and gentle through the turntable's
    plastic. I sawed down four inches, straight as I could

make it. Me and my boys—sons of cops, bookkeepers
    and ex-priests—picked up gear other DJs didn't want

no more. One prep-school kid, who just bought
    a shiny new mixer, tossed out his two-month-old

Numark which we picked from the garbage and
    hoisted home. We harvested the slider from the rich

kid's rig. I stripped the wires' tips and soldered them
    to pitch contacts. In a basement of a maple split

in Edison, NJ, we were learning to turn anything
    into anything else, while our mothers played

mah jong in the sala, and our fathers bet
    slow horses and the government bombed Iraq.

We learned to poise pennies on the cartridge head
    so the diamond stylus would sit deep in the vinyl's

groove. A dance floor could turn from winin' to riot
    quick if a record skipped when we spun back

the wax to its cue. We stayed awake from noon
    to noon, digging out from crates some forgotten

voice or violin to scratch. We juggled and chirped.
    We perfected the grind of a downbeat and dropped it

on the bassline coming around. Half trash, half
    hallelujah. Our hands cut Bach to Bambaataa

and made a dance hall jump. We held one ear
    to the syncopated kick and the other to a future

music that no one else could hear. Out of a hunk
    of rescued junk, we built a machine to mix the classics.

We faded and transformed. We chopped up masters
    and made the whole block bounce.

# Brokeheart: Just Like That

When the bass drops on Bill Withers'
"Better Off Dead," it's like 7 a.m.
and I confess I'm looking
over my shoulder once or twice
just to make sure no one in Brooklyn
is peeking into my third-floor window
to see me in pajamas I haven't washed
for three weeks before I slide
from sink to stove in one long groove
left foot first then back to the window side
with my chin up and both fists clenched
like two small sacks of stolen nickels
and I can almost hear the silver
hit the floor by the dozens
when I let loose and sway a little back
and just like that I'm a lizard grown
two new good legs on a breeze-
bent limb. I'm a grown-ass man
with a three-day wish and two days to live.
And just like that everyone knows
my heart's broke and no one is home.
Just like that, I'm water.
Just like that, I'm the boat.
Just like that, I'm both things in the whole world
rocking. Sometimes sadness is just
what comes between the dancing. And BAM!,
my mother's dead and, BAM!, my brother's
children are laughing. Just like—I can't
pop up from my knees so quick these days
and no one ever said I could sing but
tell me my body ain't good enough
for this. I'll count the aches right now,
one in each ankle, the sharp spike in my back,
this mud-muscle throbbing in my going bones.
I'm missing the six biggest screws
to hold this blessed mess together. I'm wind-

rattled. The wood's splitting. The hinges are
falling off. When the first bridge ends,
just like that, I'm a flung open door.

# Ode to the Cee-Lo Players

Any day, give me this nasty static
of street flies, this blunt smoke
ghosting overhead, this brother right here
who slaps half his rent against a brick wall
and won't flinch once though his phone's
blowing up. Right now no orchestra
of jasmine, no honey-hipped
parade could snatch him from this
huddle of petty thieves and shit talkers
trading fire. Sorrow's a kindling too.
This smoldering without wicks
becomes us. If only we didn't burn so fine
standing still, cypher where there's no truth
like a shooter's hot hand gone cold,
where you learn the rules by watching
how stones and cash trade places quick,
and some hustlers are so good
they flip the grins of giddy princes.
Know that I have crouched among boys
whose blistering wit jacks the master
alphabet the canons have handed them.
We have been the young bucks
who bear no standards and rep no set
save the galactic brotherhood
whose initiates have wrung blood
from their own sleeves into public sinks.
Here, on the avenues of chance, no one plays
alone for dollars and rocks. Our anthems
re-draw heaven, hell, and the corner shop.
We have risked more than a clutch
of crumpled singles in our fists.
This is what dice does to us. We kneel
in semicircle. We perfect the slick lean
into the toss. We hone the wrist's flick
and snap our fingers on every sweet trips-run.
Some rules you can't write down. From above,

we must sound like we're speaking in foreign
tongues. Half this game is calling out
our numbers before they even come.

# The Halo-Halo Men: An Anthem

We are the halo-halo men

the mix-mix men the fresh-cut-
mango-in-your-mouth men

The men who pee-pee in your Coke
The joke that yokes the beasts

of vinyl and diamond men
The bit-of-salt-to-cut-the-ice men

The wineskins-without-wine
blunt-hilt-of-the-bolo-to-your-head

men We are the how-how men
the carabao men back-to-ten men

Pen-pen men de sarapen
de-kutsilyo men de-alamasen

The when men Come-again men
The middle man and omega men

You build fences for we might
steal your hen men

Kimat and Pang-or men First
to suicide in the cypher men

We use our inside voices
for an outside fight men

say three Hail Mary's
and whisper Hallelujah

flip the new testament
like we do judo men

vodou men raw blood and
garlic men kilawen men

I say ag-yaman ak
you say A–

# Violets

A brisk sunset walk home: Lafayette Ave.
After weeks straight of triple layers
and double gloves, the day has inched
enough out of the freeze that I get around
just fine without my hands jammed
in my pockets and my eyes half shut
against the cold. I switchback real quick
and yank a twig jutting out from a trash can
just for kicks. I get going again, swinging the stick
as if I'm conducting this miserable choir
of pigeons at my feet. A good block to go,
I'm about to pick up the pace when I catch
a small flash of dusk out the corner of my eye,
not from the skyline but from the bit of branch
I'm holding—another violet's just sprouted
from my fist, a small flash of welts, a cluster
of indigo, a smack of dark lilac . . . which seems
to happen lately in every season. Matter of fact,
sometimes I look down the street and violets
are spilling out the doors, down the stoops,
into corners and lots. They are pooling at every curb
and mothers hang their heads out the windows
in horror. I carry the violets one by one inside
my apartment. I head straight to my kitchen
and lift the blossom to the light, roots and all,
shaking dirt loose to take a good long look
at these squares of Jesus-purple. I hold it
to my nose, say grace, and clamp my lips down
to pop a petal free. I close my mouth around it,
I pull it onto my tongue to feel its cool silk
and push it against my teeth. I chew
and chew some more and I say *why not*,
for we live in the ongoing American epoch
in which a man can shoot a child in the eye
or back and not be convicted of murder.
Who's got what magic now? Most days I am one

of the hundred million who just watches
the violets multiply. Then some nights,
I sit in my kitchen eating this one perfect flower.
Stupid, I know. But I've held things in my mouth
with more sugar and felt less blessed.
If you want to know, this violet tastes
of the slightly rotten whiff of a late April rain,
the muddy musk of old piano keys,
a dusty box emptied of nickel casings
and old colognes. It tastes a lot like
the small twitch of fog my breath makes
against my lover's belly. This flower
in case you've forgotten has sprouted
from my own fingers, maybe even deeper—
my liver, my spleen. Turns out,
rage is a flower like this one, like
that one, like this. My body's
the right mulch for it. Sometimes
a man is only as lucky as his hands.

# Wish

If the engineers manage to crunch another
hundred billion digits in their niftiest chipset yet
and craft their swiftest killing missile to date
then congratulate each other with the tiny chimes
of their slender perfect flutes, if they are paid well
and sleep well for the coming schedules of doom
and the designs down to the very joule
are symmetric and beautiful, the way hills
in the distance are sometimes symmetric
and beautiful—split down the crestline
(from birdseye)—and the laser sights' path
sweeping along them reminds us of a spine's
precision too, if the same hills are walloped
by carpet bombs, so the goats kicking their way
up the hillside are roasted by the explosion, if this
still goes on as it often does with schoolchildren
with their hands on their ears and their heads
between their knees or one hand on a rope
leading a billy goat to a patch of grass
as the rockets streak down to make war
a kind of weather, if this triple sorrow like points
of a tyrant's compass, if this battlemind, if this
*Fuckyou I'm dreaming of figs,* if this crate pushed
out the back of a truck or dropped from low-flying
planes or copters, if the children of my brother,
nonetheless, have their way with singing
and their singing means no one asks them
to pledge allegiance to fires by plucking
the fires' embers from their tongues, if this war,
I mean, this one that follows the one before it, persists,

let me not be the last to scoop
two small children, blindsided, into my arms
and feel their awkward bodies squirming
to be free, one sticking a desperate pinky up my nose
to make some space for his escape, the other, flipped

upside down, kicking me in the chin, let me know
their hip bones through their polar bear pajamas
in summer and their little teeth cracking me
on the side of the head breaking a bit of skin
above my ear as they cackle away tickled
by their unshaven lunatic uncle weeping
with joy when he finally sets them
loose on to the hardwood floor where
they tumble and wriggle like a couple ugly fish
until they grow human legs and scramble
to their brand new feet and scoot to the room
where there is a piano for them to bang on
where they can make an afternoon music
to piss their pops off mid-nap—where
they may craft the kind of nonsense
to teach kings what wicked screaming
—hoot and demonhowl and caterwaul—
two big-lunged munchkins can even make
with just their little mouths
like the sound of jet engines
winding their last time down.

# Kundiman: Hung Justice

Love, a child dreamt hard of
bread and got history

instead. Someone dreamt of
maggot-jewels in meat and

brought out blades in the name
of good science, ardor.

But who'll list kinships in
English between slaughter

and laughter? Who'll recruit
heaven's splendid refuse,

junk, our silent brigades
of busted blue-black horns,

swordless squadrons, the hum
and ruckus of strung-up

ghosts, the delirium
of angels and muddy

hilt and rust, this finch-quick
trigger, dull dagger third-

muscle deep, gas-sopped rag?
Who's got lungs for song? Hoist

not a schoolyard's one taut
noose or red bunting bloom.

My America, you
can't even love a face

as handsome as a bomb.

# Instance of an Island

One way to erase an island is to invent
a second island absolved of all the sounds
the first one ever made. We don't know
who concocted this one, where the triggerfish
and clowns fade to inky neon dashes under
a fisherman's skiff. A few plastic pontoons
knock around makeshift slips. Dusk coaxes
from the shore the small, dull chime
of a spoon against a pot and TV voices
flash slow across a cliff. Two pink lovers
in matching swimwear kiss their glasses
at the edge of a blue pool built just low enough
into the hill so the couple can gaze into the sea
and think of infinity. Many, many years ago,
a great emperor wiggled his finger
and commanded his army to corral all the lepers
in his domain then pack them into a sailing ship
to be delivered to the missions on this cluster
of verdant volcanic rock. The emperor's orders
to his captain were clear: if the monks refused
the ship's freight, the skipper was to simply
dump the whole sick cargo far from any shore.
Other incurables followed in lots over time,
or trickled in, hiding from nearby tribes,
or banished from other lands to live among these
lush slopes of mahogany, papaya, and weeds.
Two women, Filomena and Josefa, arrived
within days of one another. By then, each had lost
most their toes, though they had ten
full fingers between them, each woman
with one hand still intact. No one is sure
how it began, but once a week the pair
would knock on the door of the scowling
Madre Clementina to borrow the hospital's
only guitar, carved from jackfruit and cracked
pretty bad along the back. To these women—

no big deal, for Filomena once transcribed
the early moonlight serenades of the horny friars
in the Royal South for the brats of an Andalusian
duke. Josefa was the daughter of a carpenter,
a maker of tables to be exact. She learned
to play a harana's tremulous melodies
on her mother's banduria at the age of three.
The pair of outcasts would stifle laughs, thrilled
to earn the crusty nun's grudging *Yes,* then
amble out to lowtide and find a flat rock to share,
so they could prop the old guitar on both
their laps, the one bad wrist of each woman
unwrapped to their stumps, pulled for now
behind their backs as they looked past the bay
toward the violent waters that first carried them
here—and they jammed. Filomena with the five
deft hammers of her left and Josefa with her right,
thick-muscled—both blue-veined and furious,
scrubbing from the instrument all those wicked
rhythms from Castile to Nowhere, on a fragile
scrap of furniture that could barely hold its tune.
They sat shoulder to shoulder and thigh to thigh,
their good hands brushing from time to time.
What they couldn't remember, they made up,
and everything they made up disappeared
past the lagoon and over the ocean, every note
in every run, every lie and desire, every nick
and crack in the jackfruit, the fat harmonics
plucked from the old nun's grunts, six taut strands
of gut whose chords skimmed the water
like night locusts in bursts of low clouds
and which bore everything in front of them and behind,
the brine of the women's necks mixed with the salt
of the lagoon, the cliffs, the spoons, the bright
nimbus of the West dipping like a noose,
the future of pontoons and fake tits, the history

of nifty crowns pried loose of their jewels,
the jiggle of a little finger gone still.

One way to erase an island is to invent the waters
that surround it. You can name the waters
which will turn all the sounds the island makes into salt.
It will teach you to listen to everything you love
disappear . . . or you can invent a song so big
it will hold the entire ocean.
                    Josefa and Filomena
rocked in the dark, hip to hip, joined by that third
body of wood, which made sure there was
nothing left in the unbroken world
to possibly make them whole.

# Ten Years After My Mom Dies I Dance

The second time I learned I could take the pain
my six-year-old niece, with five cavities
humming in her teeth, lead me by the finger
to the foyer and told her dad to turn up
the Pretenders—"Tattooed Love Boys"—
so she could shimmy with me to the same jam
eleven times in a row in her princess pajamas.
When she's old enough, I'll tell her how
I bargained once with God because all I knew
of grief was to lean deep into the gas pedal
to speed down a side road not a quarter-mile
after scouring my gut and fogging my retinas
with half a bottle of cheap scotch. To those
dumb enough to take the odds against Time,
the infinite always says *You lose.* If you're lucky,
Time grants you a second chance, as I was lucky
when I got to hold the hand of my mother,
how I got to kiss that hand before I sprawled out
on the tiles of the hallway in the North Ward
so that the nurses had to step over me while
I wept. Then again, I have lived long enough
to turn on all the lights in someone else's kitchen
and move my hips in lovers' time to the same
shameless Amen sung throughout the church
our bodies build in sway. Oh magic, we move
through the universe at six hundred seventy million
miles per hour even when we are lying absolutely still.
In Brooklyn, a man can prove he's a sucker for ruin
by dropping an old school toprock on the G line
at Metropolitan despite the fifty-some strangers
all around him on the platform. Sure, I set it off
in my zipped up three-quarter coat when that big girl
opened the thunder in her lungs and let out her badass
banjo version of the Jackson 5, all of which is to say,
thank you for the kind of wacky anguish that leads me
to a sticky floor like this late-night lounge under

a century-and-a-half-old bridge where I'm about to twirl
a mostly deaf woman by the hand and listen to her whisper
a melody she's making up to a rhythm she says she feels
only through her chest, how we will hold each other
until the lights come up as if two strangers
couldn't dance this long to the same sorrows
and one body couldn't sing two songs.

# Children Walk on Chairs to Cross a Flooded Schoolyard—Taytay, Rizal Province, Philippines

*(based on the photo by Noel Celis)*

Hardly anything holds the children up, each poised
mid-air, barely the ball of one small foot
kissing the chair's wood, so
they don't just step across, but pause
above the water. I look at that cotton mangle
of a sky, post-typhoon, and presume
it's holding something back. In this country,
it's the season of greedy gods
and the several hundred cathedrals
worth of water they spill onto little tropic villages
like this one, where a girl is likely to know
the name of the man who built
every chair in her school by hand,
six of which are now arranged
into a makeshift bridge so that she and her mates
can cross their flooded schoolyard.
Boys in royal blue shorts and red rain boots,
the girls brown and bare-toed
in starch white shirts and pleated skirts.
They hover like bells that can choose
to withhold their one clear, true
bronze note, until all this nonsense
of wind and drizzle dies down.
One boy even reaches forward
into the dark sudden pool below
toward someone we can't see, and
at the same time, without looking, seems
to offer the tips of his fingers back to the smaller girl
behind him. I want the children
ferried quickly across so they can get back
to slapping one another on the neck
and cheating each other at checkers.
I've said time and time again I don't believe
in mystery, and then I'm reminded what it's like

to be in America, to kneel beside
a six-year-old, to slide my left hand
beneath his back and my right under his knees,
and then carry him up a long flight of stairs
to his bed. I can feel the fine bones,
the little ridges of the spine
with my palm, the tiny smooth stone
of the elbow. I remember I've lifted
a sleeping body so slight I thought
the whole catastrophic world could fall away.
I forget how disaster works, how it can turn
a child back into glistening butterfish
or finches. And then they'll just do
what they do, which is teach the rest of us
how to move with such natural gravity.
Look at these two girls, center frame,
who hold out their arms
as if they're finally remembering
they were made for other altitudes.
I love them for the peculiar joy
of returning to earth. Not an ounce
of impatience. This simple thrill
of touching ground.

# Ode to Eating a Pomegranate in Brooklyn

When I fall in love again I will have another heart
and a second set of eyes which is one way

to watch the woman you love      grow old

The story of my heartbreak started like this:
someone gave me a key that opens many doors

I traded it for a key that opens only one
I traded that one for another and that for another

until there were no more doors
            and I had a fist full of keys

At any given moment only part of the world is gruesome

There are three pomegranates in the fridge
waiting to be broken open

When I fall in love again
my beloved and I will spit seeds into the street

until the birds come to pluck them

When I fall in love I'll count the tick
of little pits in city puddles

I'll forget the dead
                  and count the doors instead

# You Cannot Go to the God
# You Love with Your Two Legs

And because you're not an antelope or a dog
you think you can't drop your other two limbs down
and charge toward the Eternal Heart.
But you must fall in love so deeply, those other legs
are yours too, the ones that have hauled their strange body
through a city of millions in less than a day
at its own pace, in its own pain,
and because you cannot make the pace of the one whom you love
your own and because you cannot make the pain of the one you love
your own pain, your separate aches must meet somewhere
poised in the heaven between your bodies
the skylines turned on their sides
reminders of what once was, what every man and woman
must build upon, build from, the body, the miserable,
weeping body, the deep bony awkwardness of love
in the bed. If you've kissed bricks in secret
or fallen asleep where there was no bed or spent time
lighting a fire, then you know the beginning of love
and maybe you know the end of it and maybe you know
the far ends, the doors, where loved ones enter
to check on you. It's not someone else speaking
when you hear I love you. It's only the nighttime
pouring into the breast's day. Sunset, love. The thousand
exits. The thousand ways to know your elbow
from your ass. A simple dozen troubled hunters
laying all their guns down, that one day
they may be among the first to step
into your devastated rooms
and say *Enough now, enough.*

# Brooklyn Antediluvian

The kid, no more than thirteen, backpack
slung over the shoulder, flanked by two

girls probably from his same grade
in white button-down shirts and school-

gray skirts. They walk so light, reeds ought
to be splitting this late-March breeze

so their fine stride's got the right soundtrack.
Young dude looks me up and down

in my doorway. It's about three o'clock
on Tuesday, Montrose Ave., a half-block

from the L, when most the middle school crews
come rising about five at a time from the subway.

He doesn't break his gait to point
at my I-heart-Brooklyn sweatshirt and say,

*It don't fit.* I think he means I'm too fat
for the pullover, but he says *Nah. It don't fit.*

He's not locked on my eyes for more
than a second, walking past me on Montrose—

the name of an Avenue whose two Roman
syllables imply hills and slopes banked

from foot to crest in roses and I try to conjure
not just this street but the whole borough

from East River to Kosciuszko souped-up
for miles with those prickled vines and lobes

and lobes of red. My name, in Spanish, means
rosebush. In Scotland, there's a field called Rosal—

a village sacked and looted by English dukes
so their sheep could graze on bloody grass, get fat,

then surrender their wool, hide, gristle,
and bone in anonymous service to the throne.

There are no roses there either. In Old Norse,
my name means field of horses. And maybe

there was a time those beasts galloped down
the Scottish hillocks every other day in spring,

and maybe a steaming new foal from a mare's
huffing body staggered, still sopping, into the herd.

This young brother right here swings the knot-
end of his tie from his left fist. Could be, next fall,

his good shoulders will square and the first
thin line of fuzz will etch the strong angles

of his jaw. I want to ask him, *What's your name?*
Maybe he already knows my name means

nothing. Even in a town whose backroads I know
so well I could still slip a cop tailing me twice

in one night, a town whose wooded dirt paths
beside the Northeast Corridor are narrow enough

to kiss a white girl hard and for her to bite
my skinny clavicle clean through my secondhand shirt

and for the world of New Jersey to forget that kiss ever
happened, even there, in the Borough of Bonhamtown

of Edison Township in the County of Middlesex,
where young ladies hike their skirts, drop

their green hair and skate the streets
with a backpack slung over one shoulder,

talking sweet smack until the big boys cower,
my name means nothing. Like most names,

mine was first handed down to a family
in another country whose penniless boys

had nowhere to go unless an American came
and sliced enough twenties from a wedge

to send their small, perfumed and newly bathed
crew of country-ass brown kids to rollick

with the light-skinned girls who worked
the edge of town. Then, for one night, the boys

could pay those dancers to call them whatever
they wanted. The name they gave me was

so empty you could put any landscape into it,
any country. I once put a lake inside it

and at the bottom of the water's murk,
the townspeople found a horse, just drowned.

When they cut the horse open, they found stones
the color of roses. Turns out, the stones

were worth something. So they gathered
kindling, chopped up the horse and cooked it

into a stew. The men who hauled the horse
from the water, not unlike some millions

of their time, were hungry. They dumped
the rose stones back into the lakehead

for someone else to one day harvest. And
they ate. Without a nickel to their names,

their stomachs stuffed with tough meat,
they stumbled drunk, out to the edge of town

and implored the girls to call them
John and Peter, Harry and Amoroso.

As for Montrose, I learned early on, if you follow it
far enough due north, this street changes its name.

When my mother married my father, as goes
the Western tradition, she changed her name

from Gelacio, which is Spanish, derived
from Gelasius, the Latin name of an African

pope, a Berber, they say. Look how far
a name can travel, crossing a sea borne

by a brown body whose old name
vanishes as one condition to rule

the Christian world, which he did,
according to some, with wicked orthodoxy.

I used to think the waters erased the names,
but who charts the waters charts the names

as well. The Spaniards trucked their God
from old Rome. And along with cannons

and garrotes, whetstones and coffers, Gelasius'
name was in the freight that came to a simple

village just inland from the Philippine Sea
where my mother would be born. In the end,

she lugged that name farther than Gelasius did,
from a coastal town in the tropics

to a drafty brickface with a ratty couch
and bad pipes. In Greek, her name means

full of laughter. Right now, the gleefullest
shouts bounding through the outerboroughs

belong, in part, to this kid and his two friends.
You could say, they make a sound that contains

my mother's name and I could track that
happy fracas from Bushwick to Kent and walk

far enough with them the long way toward
the Navy Yards after this block turns off, just

before they split toward their own route
home and I could stop and point out

the one-bedroom second-floor walkup
my father rented in 1964 for thirty-five dollars

a month. He paid in cash and the landlord said,
*Father, let me show you how to live.* My father

was a Father when my brother was born
and stopped being a Father when he became

a father to me—to be clear, he was a Catholic priest
until my mom got pregnant a second time.

The day my dad moved to Williamsburg, his landlord
drove him out to Chinatown and sat him at a dice game

where the puckish proprietor blew the rent
in an hour. The burly bouncers ushered the windbag

out by his elbow. My father followed. *That's
how to live, Nick.* My father's name is Nicholas,

but his family called him Charito, which is
the familiar diminutive of Rosario, or rosary,

the beads his mother held until her death,
counting the prescribed mysteries of their faith,

which has its rules, one of which is that
priests should not make love and women

should not make love to priests, but my mother
did, my father did, in secret, in the dark lots

and public parks of Chicago, until they escaped
that city's tsismis and my mother left, pregnant,

for Canada, my father landing in Brooklyn first,
in a half-bath flat on a street that trades its name

for a number before it ever reaches the river.
Brooklyn ends somewhere under water,

all the submerged wreckage joining this island
with the next. I wonder how many centuries

have left some American evidence in the name
of this thin-framed kid whose slick walk belies

the stiff green vines of the coming summer,
when his mother might call out her window for him

to set the table for dinner and some evenings
she might stay up real late waiting. I think

I know how a name can dangle mid-air as if
from a lamppost at dusk. How a mother's name

and a father's name can hang outside a window
or swing from a sad maple and no one will notice

among streetcorners first ordained in honor
of some fatcat or burning saint, but sometimes

we invent a name and its story for the hell of it,
for neither hell nor story is only ours

to remember. Here's proof: There once was a man
who put on a crown and made himself a king.

And his first order from the throne was to send
his governors out to issue new names

to each town. Among the hungry was a woman
who lived so long that, for generations, she

watched over the land upon which
thousands of wild horses stampeded, where

her whole tribe had built their homes, in which
they made love and broke each other's noses

and the horses snorted down from the hills'
crests every week of every decade of her life

and not once did she bear witness to a steed
mid-gallop flopped over so fast and so hard

it should open like a sudden rose, let alone
the gore of a hundred, of ten thousand. How

does a name become a field of beasts
become a field of flowers? How does any

such flood alter a field in secret and how
should an ancient field conceal the way

we say our original names? The woman.
those horses, the brutal floral funk that spells

a meadow long after the animals are gone?
I like to believe you can teach a child

to snip a blossom from a bloody thicket.
I like to believe you can learn to pinch

that simple bud, hold it to your lips, and
invoke the billion hidden names trilling within.

So when you join a dozen or one hundred
village elders, armed with small sickles,

having gathered from so many forgotten fields
some strange species of equine blossom,

you will place the flowers upon the dumb
governors' tables, which were first hewn,

hammered, and hand-lacquered by men
and women who never sat to eat—neither

simple meal nor feast. Listen:
                              our names

were taken. And in their place the bastards
shoved some other word like *laughter*

crafted with a Spanish hatchet or carved
like a joke into Roman stone. Every name

is a word embedded with a wish. Empire
is a word. Equinox is a word. In our time

you might see the sickles swarm in flowing
metallic droves to cut lost names from a field

of prickled stalks. You might see multitudes
come, not to watch the field but to reclaim it,

to slash a path all the way back to the tables
we first fashioned, to present our gruesome

harvest to our governors who—no surprise—
refuse to listen. To those ghastly murmurs

culled from the grisly pastures, that roll call
of the dying and nearly dead, they just

plug their ears with their fine royal wool.
                          Oh, Montrose,
four stops from the river and six from Union Square,

the woman who kept watch over the horses,
lived long enough to take her name back.

She whispered it into the field and the field
said the word over and over into its own deep dirt

and rock and billion-gnarl until the name
stayed for good, coded into its light at dusk.

There's a herd of bloody brutes that blossomed
before her eyes and here arrives your summer

child at my twenty-first century door,
late-March, the winter still stiffening our toes.

When I was a young man, I once had fifty singles
in my pocket. I thought I'd get to keep my name

from birth by writing it on dollar bills
or slipping those notes one by one across a bar

into the fingers of a woman working
the afternoon set among the turnpike

semis across the Hudson. It was enough
to pay for a couple drinks and an hour

to chat with a girl in pasties and a thong.
Like my father I thought I had nowhere

else to go. So in dirty cutoffs and flip flops
I followed desperate boys half way around

the world into the red light districts
where dozens of girls in riding boots or

stilettos scanned us for a balikbayan
(dipshit American? Even better.),

where you can choose a name
and lose your face in flashing neon.

But you have to remember the name
they gave you first. The one you came with.

My cousin, a younger man than me,
told me: if you manage to escape

any darkness (say a haunted grove
or thick wooded stretch patrolled by enemy

soldiers), right away, you have to turn
toward the dark. You have to shout

your own name back to make sure
your soul follows you into daylight

or at least into some dim street. You see,
that dark could belong to a precinct of captive

dancers, where, with your last fifty greenbacks,
you're supposed to order endless beers

and the girls will hug you all night and make you
think you're inventing a language to kiss them—

and another language to lie in bed
until dawn mostly alone—but those

women know the slick talk of every john
from Melbourne to Mississippi.

One morning I tipped the madame and flagged
a taxi bloodshot. A light rain spat down.

Back at my uncle's house, I thought
it might be beautiful to shut the blinds

and listen to the tapping as it steadied,
heavy on the corrugated roofs

through night into the next morning,
the slow gathering of a trillion hammers

spiking the metal overhead, not one
wind in the streets. The sewer line out

near the national highway and the six-block
gash in the blacktop under repair filled quick

with rain, chasing the mice into every bedroom.
I might not get to the body count the typhoon

left behind, how it circled back, zig-zagged
for a second rip-and-run across the island.

Let's just say they baptize natural disasters
as if we could call them closer or coax them back

to where they come from: Katrina, Sandy, Ondoy.
During that last storm, it took two weeks

before the worst of the waters receded,
before they found three men rotting in a tree.

No one had looked up. But for the sweet
reek wafting down, no one would have seen them

drowning in the sky. It's what happens when
a storm keeps stirring a river and a river

keeps taking, flushing shanties down main roads
towing more than 3,000 bodies below.

Even the governor's snorting horses flopped
onto their sides, the tonnage whisked off

tumbling in the current and I'll save the story
of the yard-hand who hid a sack of stolen

stones and their scarlet glow, how he shoved them
over the course of weeks before the storm

into the mouth of his master's favorite parade horse
suffering from colic. The floods

left the boy and took the horse.
                                    Metropolis,
do you hear me? Young man? I don't want

anything. I want this. I want to say
the names we've been given aloud. The ones

they took away. I want to shout out the names
of those who named us. I want to go back

far enough that all of memory gets cloudy
and we have to—as our grandfathers

and grandmothers have done for more
than four hundred years—make it up,

even if all we got now is the whiff of a river
swelling, the half-truths and full lies inscribed

in books packed in a middle-school satchel
on a cool day in Brooklyn. I live

in a country where the legends
are illegible or torn off. I wake up

on a block where I can watch from a distance
100,000 billboards alter the nighttime

sky, the kind of lights that could change
the bodies of horses in a field before

your very eyes, dashing down a meadow,
the thorns burst from their rumps

and mouths and undersides blooming bloody.
What do I know anyway... I'm the one

who believes we have ancient names
like dawnlight flashing into the dreams

of murderers and sunken into the hillsides
of countries whose shanties and projects

are named for moguls and saints, though
children drown here, just like they do

everywhere: Manila, New Orleans,
Brooklyn. There's not a name that fits.

You could flood an avenue with storm-
water or roses or the horses could suddenly

split down their bellies mid-stampede.
Your name could curse a city. And it would be

a calamity. It would be spring.

# ACKNOWLEDGMENTS

I am grateful to you, Mary Rose Go, singer, gardener, steward of Jersey kalo, hunter of lamok, for your care and your questions, for your listening, for your practice, for the openness of your sorrow and your laughter, for the sudden dances in our dining room, for the shared meals and separate ones, too, for your joy in the land, in water, for your courage and your tenderness, I'm blessed to build a home and a life with you; Aracelis Girmay and Ross Gay, there's virtually nothing in this book without you, nothing without your intelligence and love; Curtis Bauer, hombre de varios mundos, hermano, compañero en mi camino; Idoia Elola; John Murillo, Nicole Sealey, Tyehimba Jess, A. Van Jordan, Willie Perdomo, you already know, mi gente; Jessica Hagedorn; Quincy Troupe; Randall Horton; Tim Seibles; Fish Vargas; Latasha Nevada Diggs; Krista Franklin; Afaa Michael Weaver; Dwayne Betts; Greg Pardlo; Mitchell Jackson; Major Jackson; Stairwell across time and space; David Wright Faladé; Cristina Ali Farah; Paul Lisicky; Janice Sapigao; Melissa Sipin; Ama Codjoe; Steve Scafidi; Tracy K. Smith; Wendy Walters; Lynne Procope; Bassey Ikpi; Syreeta McFadden; Jennifer Chang; Eric Gamalinda; Rich Villar; Jake Camacho; Christine Balance; Gayle Romasanta; Dawn Mabalon; our manongs, especially those who welcomed me in Delano; Christian Campbell; Elizabeth Alexander; Cheryl Boyce-Taylor; Abena Koomson-Davis; Sabrina Hayeem-Ladani; Kamilah Aisha Moon; Rachel Eliza Griffiths; Roger Bonair-Agard, Mathilda De Dios, Uma, Nina, and Arima; Jason Bayani; Mama Edna Mancao; Stacey Young; Sara Yukimoto-Saltman; Marie Howe; Jason Koo; Fish Vargas; BJ Ward; my colleagues at the Institute for the Study of Global Racial Justice — Erica Armstrong Dunbar, Elise Boddie, and Michelle Stephens; Ron Villanueva; Joseph Legaspi; Sarah Gambito; Jon Pineda; Aimee Nezhukumatathil; Oliver de la Paz; Vijay Seshadri; Tiphanie Yanique; Eliel Lucero; Roberto Carlos Garcia; Darla Himeles; Lynne McEniry; Ysabel Gonzalez; Michelle Greco; Malik Abduh; Sevé Torres; Cynthia Dewi Oka; Jeff Kass; Angel Nafis; Cleon Reid; Hector Hernandez; Aiza Galdo; Junot Díaz; Monica Malamug; Phil Malamug; Junji Malamug;

Jojo Malamug; Kristen Lee; Sheri Haili, Bob Chaleunvong, and Kyson Kapono; Jing Yang; Kelly McDonald; Robin Margolis; Janelle Grace; Roxanne and Ray Nepomuceno; Harry Jenkins; Steve Mallorca; Gina Apostol; Lara Stapleton; Nina Noveno; Evelina Galang; Terrance Hayes; Chris Abani; Suzanne Gardinier; Patricia Smith; Cherita Harrell; Micaiah Johnson; Paul Genega; Leslie Shipman; Keith Green; Aaron Hostetter; Shanyn Fiske; Tim Lynch; Marissa Johnson Valenzuela; Ayinde Merrill; Paul Simmons; Alicia Ostriker; Jeet Thayil; Krip Yuson; Auntie Shrinah Henderson; Uncle Jerry; Auntie Karen; Jerry Boy, Sara, and the rest of the Mancao 'ohana; Nicholas Anthony and Heidi Loder-Rosal; Patricia Walling; Joy Quides; Tita Candi; Albert and Katherine Cabassa; Mark Rosal; Milo and Remi; Joyce; Christine Calura, Tony Dozier, Kalesi; my dad; Tita Thelma; Uncle José and Auntie Vee; Uncle Charlie and Auntie Celia; Uncle Naro and Auntie Toring; Tita Grace; Yenz, Ed, and kids; Louie, Shane, and kids; George Narciso; Manang Ilyn; Manong Amado; Rosemarie; James; Emy; Edmond; Jay; our whole Narciso-Gelacio family from Balacad to Hawai'i to California to Chicago to NYC/NJ; Yuri and Vovo; to Sylvia, Guillermo, Enrique, and Melinda Huezo—thanks to everyone who has touched my life in countless meaningful ways.

I want to acknowledge the time and resources afforded me by the John Simon Guggenheim Foundation; the Lannan Residency in Marfa; Civitella Ranieri; and Rutgers Research Council grants.

I also want to thank Dore A. Minatodani, Jodie Mattos, and the rest of the staff at the Thomas Hale Hamilton Library at the University of Hawai'i at Mānoa; Zara Wilkinson at Rutgers-Camden's Paul Robeson Library; as well as the staffs at the Founders Library at Howard University, the Ayer Collection at the Newberry Library, and the Field Museum.

I want to further thank Gabriel Fried, my editor, and publishers Karen and Michael Braziller for supporting this work for almost two decades now.

Poems from *Uprock Headspin Scramble and Dive* originally appeared in *Lumina, Folio, Sarah Lawrence Review, Columbia: A Journal of Literature and Art, The Literary Review, North American Review, Babaylan Speaks*, and the anthologies *Beacon Best 2001, Screaming Monkeys*, and *Eros Pinoy*.

Poems from *My American Kundiman* originally appeared in *Vespertine, ABZ, Risen from East, North American Review, Brevity, Boxcar, Sow's Ear, Pindeldyboz*.

Poems from *Boneshepherds* originally appeared in *American Poetry Review, The Collagist, Solstice, Crab Orchard Review, Diode, Harvard Review, Indiana Review, The Literary Review, Mascara, New Orleans Review, Ninth Letter, Otoliths, Tin House, Tulaan Sa Tren, Washington Square.*

Poems from *Brooklyn Antediluvian* originally appeared in *Alaska Quarterly Review, Ampersand Review, Apogee, At Length, The Collagist, Exit 7, Four Way Review, Gulf Coast, Mead, New England Review, Poetry,* Poets.org, *Southern Illinois Review, Tin House, Union Station Magazine, Waxwing.*

"You Cannot Go to the God You Love with Your Two Legs" was reprinted in *Best American Poetry.*

New poems in this collection originally appeared in *Buzzfeed, Poems for Kobe* (presented to Kobe Bryant in his last game against the Brooklyn Nets before he retired), *American Poetry Review, Rattle, Ampersand Review, The Collagist, Virginia Quarterly Review.* "A Preface" originally appeared in *LitHub.*